PERFORMANCE³

PLANNING × PEOPLE × PROCESS

L. Gary Boomer, CPA, CITP

Synergetic Publications, Inc.
Nashville, Tennessee

Synergetic Publications, Inc.
P.O. Box 1506
Hendersonville, Tennessee 37077-1506

ISBN 0-9632248-0-8

Synergetic Publications, Inc. has produced this edition of
PERFORMANCE³ in conjunction with
Boomer Consulting Inc.
610 Humboldt Street, Manhattan, Kansas 66502
1-888-266-6375

Book Design: Bozeman Design, Franklin, Tennessee
Manufactured in the United States of America

DEDICATION

To my parents, Warren and Vi Boomer who provided great support and a positive attitude. I wish they were still here.

CONTENTS

ACKNOWLEDGEMENTS   vii
INTRODUCTION   ix

Part I: PLANNING

Chapter 1   A Shared Services or Shared Vision Firm   3
2   The ROI on Thinking and Planning   9
3   The Process of Planning   15
4   Conducting a Successful Summit   25

Part II: PEOPLE

Chapter 5   The Evolution of Partner Value   35
6   Building Your Team   41
7   The Training/Learning Culture   47
8   Identifying Transformation Agents   53
9   Retention and Attraction Strategies   59
10   Selecting Firm Leaders   69
11   Holding Your Managing Partner Accountable   73

Part III: PROCESSES

Chapter 12 Improve Processes and Profits   83
13   Globalization — The Impact on Processes   89
14   The Challenges of Digital Content Management   95
15   IT Governance, Focus and Evaluation   101
16   Prescription for the Profession   107

Part IV: PERFORMANCE³

Chapter 17 Exponential Results – 10 Times Growth   113
18   Ten Rules of Technology Management   121
19   The Compensation Challenge   127
20   Gratitude & Celebration   141

ACKNOWLEDGEMENTS

This book would not have happened without the support and assistance of my associates at Boomer Consulting, Inc.

Steve Blundell, Don Hunt, Larry Wolf and Nils Thompson are great friends and all were inspirational in my move from a partner in a regional CPA firm to consulting, speaking and writing.

Dan Sullivan, founder of the Strategic Coach Program, has provided me with coaching and confidence over the past 12 years. Not only has he helped with balance — he has taught me about packaging intellectual property which has allowed Boomer Consulting to become an intellectual capital company. The Strategic Coach program continues to support Boomer Consulting in our vision to guide the transformation of the accounting industry by providing visionary leadership, advisory services and knowledge-based products.

Charlie Flood has also provided intellectual property and capital coaching and managed the production of this book.

The accounting and consulting professions have provided many great experiences and relationships.

Other members of The Advisory Board have been most supportive and provided great counsel — including Jay Nisberg, Allan Koltin, and Gary Shamis. Don Istvan, Jeff Salins, Chris Frederiksen, Don Scholl, Bob Martin, Jeff Pawlow and Troy Waugh have also been influential and supportive in my career.

To all of the above and the many clients I have had the opportunity to serve, I am most grateful and trust these experiences will provide value to those who are serious about improving performance for themselves, their firms and their clients.

Finally, I would like to thank my wife Mary and our children Jeff, Jim and Katie for their support and tolerance of my continual travel.

INTRODUCTION

According to the latest edition of the Merriam-Webster™ dictionary, a *principle* is defined as "a comprehensive and fundamental law, doctrine, or assumption" while a *formula* is defined as "a recipe or prescription." One must consider fundamentals when it comes to improving, growing and developing a differentiating business culture. Prestigious management conferences often focus on so called "silver bullets" ranging from marketing to information technology in their search for the right formula.

Until now, nobody has offered a business formula or principle that demonstrates the dynamic interaction of the three most important components. People × Planning × Process equals PERFORMANCE³. Being able to communicate such a formula so it is understood by the entire organization is as important as the formula.

The simultaneous focus on:
- People,
- Planning,
- And processes

results in:

- Incremental growth,
- A transformed culture
- Exponential growth

...PERFORMANCE³

These are the exponential results that businesses strive for in their quest for excellence.

Focusing on any one *best practice* may result in incremental growth. However, "incremental growth" is just not enough in today's knowledge and wisdom-based economy — while "exponential growth" is impossible without changes in mind-sets, strategies, skills, tools and culture.

Today there is PERFORMANCE³ — Planning × People × Process, — a proven formula. Other management topics such as marketing and technology are simply components of the formula. As with any formula, the ingredients must be added proportionately, and timing is of utmost importance.

Firms today are faced with a fork in the road. Either they choose mediocrity and commoditization — or excellence and unique processes that create new value. Excellence requires a new way of thinking, new strategies, new skills and new tools. Excellence focuses on the unique abilities of people and their significance to the company's strategic plan. Old paradigms must be broken in order to experience exponential improvement and growth. Are your people on the income statement or balance sheet? Most businesses put their people on the income statement while they capitalize technology on the balance sheet. Does this make sense to you?

Looking Ahead with Confidence

Likewise, owners spend little or no time planning and thinking about how their organizations will look in three to five years. Just as importantly is how individuals fit into the company's strategic game plan. At best you may conduct an annual firm summit, but generally there is little or no accountability after the summit. Goals too often turn into dreams rather than reality. In fact, most organizations refer to this process as a "retreat". A *retreat* focuses on the past rather than the future. *Worrying* about dangers is much different than spending time *thinking* about strategies to overcome obstacles and avoid risks. It isn't easy; planning and thinking take most people out of their comfort zone.

At any given point, a business has a group of people (resources).

- Are they the right ones?
- Do they fit with the company's strategic plan?
- Where are their strengths?
- Where are their weaknesses?
- What are their unique *abilities*?

- Does the business need talent it currently doesn't have?
- Does it have talent it doesn't need or is obsolete?
- What is the return on training and learning?
- Is there a marketing and sales culture?

What differentiates great firms from mediocre ones is whether leadership ignores or addresses these questions.

What if your company was 10 times larger than it is today? What would the company have to do differently? What would *you* have to do differently? Should you start doing those things today if your company is only growing at 10-15%?

The Process Trap

Merriam-Webster™ defines "process" as a series of actions or operations conducing to an end. Most businesses are caught in the process trap, but are their processes efficient?

- What is the impact of technology on their processes?
- Are they using technology as an accelerator or is it disabling?
- What controls do they have over their processes?
- When was the last time the processes were reviewed?
- Why don't they spend time on process improvement?
- Are the processes documented so they can be a part of the company's orientation and training program?
- Are the processes being adhered to? (quality control)

It is easy to get caught in *doing* rather than *improving* because current compensation formulas are generally outdated. Processes are not enough. PERFORMANCE³, combines planning, people and processes. It allows businesses to grow exponentially. The world saw incremental growth from the industrial to the information age. Today we are transforming to the age of wisdom, and some will experience merely incremental growth again. But you must be able to see the big picture if you desire to grow.

Join the Major Leagues

This book discusses the strategies, skills, tools and the coaching necessary to overcome your obstacles and experience exceptional improvement, a transformed culture, and exponential growth. The choice is yours. At what level do you want to play?

Part I

PLANNING

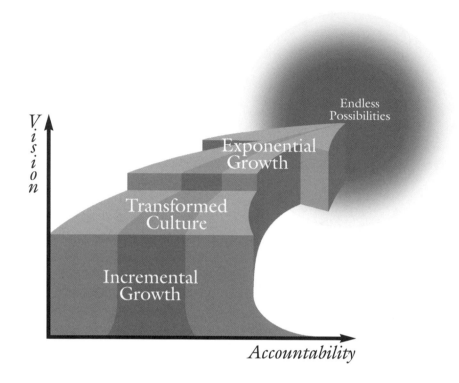

PLANNING×PEOPLE×PROCESS

Exponential Growth
Transformed Culture
Incremental Growth

Chapter 1

A SHARED SERVICES
OR SHARED VISION FIRM

Professional service companies can be successful as either *shared services or shared vision* firms. You might be asking the question: "Why should this simple distinction make a difference?" As long as your understanding is consistent, one way or the other, it might not make a difference, although there are some natural limitations to *shared services* firms.

To determine whether your firm is a *shared services or shared vision* business, conduct an honest assessment of your firm's orientation. Once you have taken this step the next logical step is to develop a strategic plan. We will discuss this process later in the book.

While *shared services* firms can grow and prosper financially, *shared vision* firms can provide more than just financial results. *Shared vision* firms can also provide the potential for exponential growth as well as a differentiating culture where individuals are rewarded for their significance in support of the firm's strategic objectives. A *shared vision* firm consistently provides direction, growth potential, integration with each member's personal goals and a differentiating culture.

The following questions will assist you in determining where your firm is today. *Shared services* firms are limited to incremental improvement and growth, but *shared vision* firms can achieve overall firm improvement, exponential growth and a differentiating culture.

In order to maximize growth, partnerships must change their management orientation. Firms interested in exponential growth should seriously consider the merits of PERFORMANCE³ thinking — Planning, People and Processes. In addition to the three areas of focus, there are three levels of development for firms using the PERFORMANCE³ Process. P1 is firm improvement, P2 is the creation of a differentiating culture and finally P3 is exponential growth.

Orientation Questions

Question	Yes	No
1. Does your firm have a strategic plan with buy-in from the owners and staff?		
2. Does your firm have a professional management team?		
3. Is your firm managed by a CEO or Managing Partner?		
Are owners compensated for objectives other than financial (charge hours and book of business)?		
4. Firm and office management?		
5. Development of staff and other owners?		
6. Management of staff and other owners?		
7. Client development and satisfaction?		
8. Process improvement and innovation?		
9. Does your firm have succession and retirement plans in place?		
10. Does your firm view technology as a strategic asset and accelerator?		
11. Does your firm have written standards, policies and procedures?		
12. If so, do the firm owners comply with the standards, policies and procedures?		

Yes to 9 or more of the questions — your are on your way to becoming a *shared vision firm*. Yes to 6-8 of the questions — you are in transition. Yes to 5 or less of the questions, you are a *shared services* firm.

While the benefits of being a *shared vision* firm are great and the dangers associated with a *shared services* firm are significant, both have the potential for financial success. The fundamental problem with *shared services* firms is they tend to be about the owners, rather than the firm. With most of the controls and systems designed to manage costs and build shareholder value, it is difficult to sustain systemic growth — and even more difficult to achieve exponential growth in a *shared services* firm. Lack of succession and continuity is also a risk of a *shared services* firm. It takes planning, processes and the right people to be a *shared vision* firm. The interests of the firm must come first. Once you have determined where you are today and where you want to be in three years, you can then begin implementing the appropriate strategies.

Many firms won't fall neatly into one catagory, and some are striving for transition. But the following table illustrates some of the key differences between the two types of firms:

Organizational Behavior Table
Shared Services or *Shared Vision*

Shared Services Firm	Issue	Shared Vision Firm
MP- Executive Committee	Governance	CEO-Managing Partner
Little time for planning & thinking	Planning – Strategic, IT, HR, Succession, Staff Development	Yes, integrated partner & staff game plans
Book of business then the firm – Owners in charge of key leadership roles	Management Focus	Professionals in key leadership roles — CEO, CFO, CIO, HR, Marketing, etc.
Protect individuals	Agreements	Protect the firm & owners

Unfunded, often unrealistic	Retirement	Funded or unfunded, but limited
No plan - hope to hire future leadership	Succession	On going development of leaders
Overhead	Technology	Strategic asset
Focus on CPE requirements	Training & Learning	Technical CPE, soft skills, & leadership management
Charge hours and book of business	Owner Compensation	Goal oriented, Balanced Scorecard
Multiple processes that are generally not adhered to by owners	Standards, Policies & Procedures	Documented and adhered to by everyone

PERFORMANCE[3] can transform your firm; however it requires a proper balance between planning and processes. Then, as Jim Collins points out in his book *Good to Great,* you'll have "the right people in the right seats on the bus."

Now that you have a better sense of your orientation, you can begin the thinking necessary to develop a plan for exponential growth. The remainder of this section will focus on the planning process in general with an eye toward new levels of growth and business performance.

It all starts with some serious thinking. *Shared Services or Shared Vision?* At what level do you wish to play? The choice is yours!

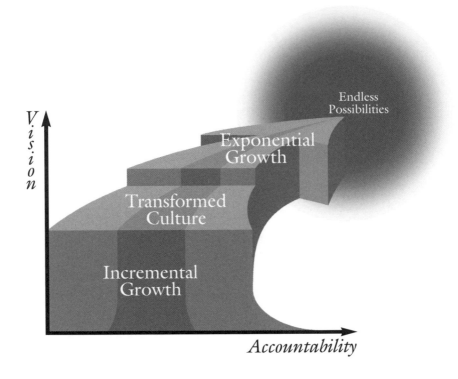

PLANNING × PEOPLE × PROCESS

Exponential Growth
Transformed Culture
Incremental Growth

Chapter 2

THE ROI ON THINKING
AND PLANNING

Do your partners have time to *think,* or are they only focused on their books of business and charge hours? Most successful firms *think* differently than ordinary firms. They also value the thinking process and make time for multiple types of thinking. To change your firm, you must change the thinking of its partners. This isn't an easy task given that most leaders do not embrace change. Therefore, most partners focus on the things that drive compensation, and little time is spent thinking and planning. If this describes your firm, read on about the differences between firm leadership/management and client service partners.

The following exercise will help you identify the differences as well as demonstrate the importance of thinking and planning.

Step 1

John C. Maxwell in *Thinking For A Change* lists several types of thinking. Identify the top three that describe the majority of your client service partners.

- ❏ Bottom-line
- ❏ Strategic
- ❏ Possibility
- ❏ Realistic
- ❏ Creative
- ❏ Popular
- ❏ Shared
- ❏ Reflective
- ❏ Focused
- ❏ Big-Picture

Step 2

Now identify the three words that best describe your firm's
leadership group.

- ❏ Bottom-line
- ❏ Strategic
- ❏ Possibility
- ❏ Realistic
- ❏ Creative
- ❏ Popular
- ❏ Shared
- ❏ Reflective
- ❏ Focused
- ❏ Big-Picture

Step 3

Identify the words that best describe your thinking.

- ❏ Bottom-line
- ❏ Strategic
- ❏ Possibility
- ❏ Realistic
- ❏ Creative
- ❏ Popular
- ❏ Shared
- ❏ Reflective
- ❏ Focused
- ❏ Big-Picture

*Chances are most of your production partners will be described as
bottom-line, focused, realistic and reflective.* Hopefully your firm
leadership group can be described with words like *strategic,
creative, big-picture and possibility.*

While these methods of thinking are not mutually exclusive, they
point to significant differences among partners and the need to
communicate and build consensus. The time to do this is normally

looked at as non-chargeable and therefore non-productive. But this begs the question: Is this a problem with thinking or with the firm's value system?

As firms grow, they place greater value on leadership, management, and planning. Often in smaller firms the entire focus is on book of business and charge hours. While these are important, they are the expected results of efficient standards, policies, procedures, satisfied clients and a learning/training culture. In other words, your firm needs balance in order to maximize its performance. Balance is also required in order to retain and attract quality people.

If current *thinking* is a problem, how does it impact growing firms? I believe current partner compensation formulas are generally outdated and need to be replaced with the Balanced Scorecard and pay for performance systems. In order to accomplish this, new *thinking* is required at all levels of the firm.

Most people are motivated to think for three different reasons: *pain, education and reward.* Because so many firms have been successful it is a challenge to get many partners to think about the future even though they know that significant changes are ahead. These changes are primarily due to increased regulation, an increasing lack of qualified people and commoditization of many traditional services. All of these changes have the potential for pain, learning and rewards — which will invariably cause people to think.

How somebody thinks may be quite different due to his or her position in the firm. Firms should be able to communicate a vision of what they will look like in 3-5 years, define objectives and identify initiatives and strategies to meet the objectives. This is all part of the strategic planning process. Many firm leaders say their firms are already doing this. To this I say, "Great, but are your partners really committed to thinking and acting like the future firm or the firm of the past?"

Many people in our profession started in firms that were much smaller and less regulated. Today, most of those firms have grown significantly. Some of this growth is internal, while some comes by acquisition and mergers. Most people are capable of thinking differently in terms of a larger organization, but some simply choose not to. Thus, management is forced to coach these people to the next level or counsel them out of the firm. While counseling a person out of the firm goes against *popular* thinking, the end result is that both the person and firm generally benefit from this action.

Here are some suggested actions to improve the *"thinking"* in your firm:

1. Conduct annual, seperate planning summits (Strategic, Technology, Human Resources, Training/Learning, Compensation and Succession)

2. Reward people for participating in the summits

3. Utilize the Balanced Scorecard for determining compensation

4. Foster an atmosphere for thinking — and budget time for it

5. Provide education and consistent communication about the firm's vision and strategic initiatives

6. Measure progress on a quarterly basis through 90-Day Accountably Reviews

While these six steps sound simple, their execution requires leadership, discipline and follow-through. Thinking and planning save time as well as produce better results. Focusing on results rather than effort (hours) is a concept that will improve performance and the marketability of your firm.

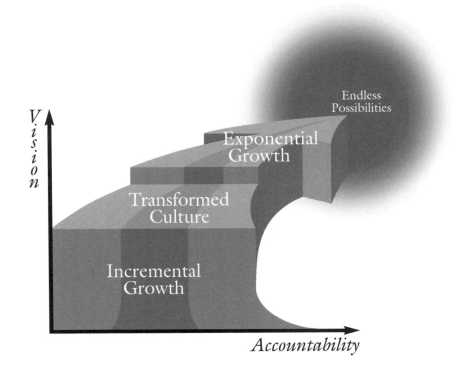

PLANNING × PEOPLE × PROCESS

Exponential Growth
Transformed Culture
Incremental Growth

Chapter 3

THE PROCESS OF PLANNING

It is often said that the process is more important than the plan when it comes to strategic planning. I agree that the process is important, but without a strategic plan, firms severely limit their potential. The process does take time, and as a result many accounting firms never get around to developing a strategic plan. There are plenty of excuses why firms fail to do this, but none can justify operating without a plan in today's rapidly changing business environment. By going without a strategic plan, many firms operate without consensus and a lack of a shared vision. Additionally, they often spread their resources too thin to have an impact. Without a plan, partners and staff can easily avoid accountability. The PERFORMANCE³ model addresses all of these issues and more.

Let's look at team sports for an analogy. What would you think of a coach who prepared his team for each week's game without a game plan? What if no score was kept? Most of you would think that foolish and the chances of success slim even if the coach had quality players. Let's face the facts most small to mid-sized firms don't have all the star players, and all admit that they have limited resources. Similarly, it makes sense for firms to develop a strategic plan and to utilize some of the tools available to reduce time required in the strategic planning process.

Let's quickly review the steps:

- Define the vision
- Develop a mission statement
- Agree on core values
- Develop strategic objectives
- Identify measurements of success
- Determine strategic initiatives
- Assign responsible parties and due dates

These steps must be followed if firms want to operate as a team and at peak performance. In many firms, individual visions and goals often conflict with those of the firm.

The partnership form of governance has contributed to many of the problems faced by the accounting profession over the past thirty years. Partners believe they have the right to participate and an obligation to debate key decisions. But this often contributes to inconsistencies and even insubordination in some firms. Given these circumstances, firms need a method to quickly develop a vision, mission statement, core values, strategic plan, core processes, policies and procedures. Think of the sports analogy previously mentioned. A coach needs to quickly develop a game plan, communicate the plan and prepare for competition by practicing. How many of your partners and staff know and agree with the firm's current game plan? Successful communcation can occur in a CPA firm if it has the right leadership (Coach) and players who desire to play as a team rather than rugged individuals.

Here are some of the tools to help you reduce the time requirements:

Tool	Time Requirement	Benefit
*The Positive Focus Exercise™	1 hour	Determines strengths and maintains confidence
*DOS Exercise™	1 hour	Quickly identifies major dangers, opportunities & strengths
*The 10 Times Growth Model™	1 hour	Identifies firm requirements and, more importantly, personal requirements
The Upside Down Budget	1 hour	Builds partner consensus over growth, compensation and required overhead
The One-Page Laminated Game Plan – Side One Side Two	4 hours 4 hours	Records vision, mission, core values and strategic objectives; Lists strategic initiatives, responsible parties and due dates i.e. ACCOUNTABILITY

*The Positive Focus™, The DOS Exercise™, and The 10 Times Growth Model™ are all tools developed and produced by The Strategic Coach Program™.

Developing a plan and building consensus are just the first steps in the process. Someone must manage the plan and hold people accountable. This requires time and "edge." "Edge" is simply the ability and willingness to make tough decisions (yes or no). It is difficult to have time and edge if you are focused on client service and charge hours. Too many firms avoid tough decisions and controversy because they are organized as a partnership. The fastest growing firms who attract the brightest people are aligned and have great leadership (vision) and management (discipline).

Leaders chase vision while managers chase goals. Someone must be working on the future firm while others work on the current firm. Problems arise when partners and personnel focus on the firm of the past. This is human nature and difficult to avoid because most people prefer to focus on the present or the past. Few have the ability and desire to focus on the future firm because it requires vision, acceptance of change and risk. As we all know, accountants by nature are risk adverse.

Take the following steps if you don't have a strategic plan but desire to start operating at a higher level – to move from Incremental Growth to Transformational Culture.

1. Hire an experienced facilitator with accounting firm experience. Don't attempt this on your own. Provide key financial and biographical information on key personnel to the facilitator prior to the strategic planning meeting.

2. Set dates for a two-day strategic planning meeting.
   a. Utilize the morning of day one to build consensus among owners.
   b. Utilize the afternoon of day one to identify and prioritize strategic initiatives that align with the firm's vision and core values.
   c. Avoid tactical discussions.
   d. Involve other key personnel and staffing in this session.
   e. Ask the facilitator or firm administrator to develop a one page game plan on the morning of day two.
   f. Present the one-page game plan to owners and key

personnel on day two during the afternoon.
g. Make appropriate modifications to the plan.

3. Consistently and repeatedly communicate the plan to all personnel.

4. Require owners and staff to complete quarterly game plans that align with the firm's game plan. These should be reviewed and approved by appropriate personnel.

5. Continue the process quarterly until it becomes a profitable habit.

6. Annually review and update the plan.

This process is bound to change the culture of your firm resulting in a move to the next level — a transformed culture. Some will resist, but leadership must stay the course. Those who continue to resist should be terminated. Staff may initially question your commitment to the process but will quickly accept change if you consistently communicate and follow through. Partner resistance is normal. Many partners do not want change, especially if it impacts their routine and/or earnings. Just remember that all progress starts with the truth!

Jones & Company, LLP
Strategic Game Plan

Vision

- Jones & Company, LLP will be the major firm in the Kansas City region offering quality service to small and medium businesses and their owners.

Core Values

- Client relationships
- Integrity and honesty
- Preparedness
- Personal development
- Respect and teamwork
- Accountability/Responsibility
- Rapid adoption of new processes & technologies

Mission Statement

- Jones & Company, LLP is dedicated to implementing strategies that enhance the well being of our people and the clients we serve.

Strategic Objectives

- Enhance the success of the firm and its employees.
- Improve the firm's succession and retirement plans.
- Develop and maintain the firm's technology in order to provide a strategic competitive advantage.
- Implement a firm learning/training program in order to hire and retain quality personnel.
- Enhance the one-firm concept and develop a firm culture based upon teamwork.

Strategic Obj.	Measurement	Due Date	Assigned To
1. Enhance the success of the firm and its employees.	• % growth in annual revenue • Growth in annual profitability • % of staff achieving professional certifications • Staff retention rates • Comparison to peer firm statistics in Boomer Circles	9/30/20xx 12/30/20xx 3/31/20xx 6/30/20xx See objective #4.	CEO - Partners CEO – Executive Committee CEO – PICs Marketing Director
2. Improve the firm's succession and retirement plans.	• Completion of a written plan • Successful retirement of one or more owners • % Funding of plans	12/31/20xx 12/31/20xx 3/31/20xx 10/31/20xx 6/30/20xx 6/30/20xx	CEO – Legal Counsel CEO – Firm Adm. Task Force Task Force Owner Firm Adm. Firm Adm.
3. Develop and maintain the firm's technology in order to provide a strategic competitive advantage.	• % of net revenue invested annually • Amount invested per FTE • Increase in revenue per FTE	9/30/20xx 10/15/20xx ASAP 6/30/20xx 9/31/20xx 12/31/20xx	CEO – Firm Leaders CEO-HR Partner & IT Leader Task Force Task Force Task Force
4. Implement a firm learning /training program in order to hire and retain quality personnel.	• Evaluation of personal training requirements for each employee as a benchmark. • Report on number of courses completed • Surveys of personnel • Focus group feedback	9/30/20xx 6/30/20xx 12/31/20xx 10/15/20xx 9/30/20xx 12/31/20xx	CEO – HR Learning Director Task Force Learning Director/Key Personnel IT Director
5. Enhance the one-firm (Shared Vision) concept and develop a firm culture based upon teamwork.	• Compliance with firm policies and procedures • Success of firm sabbatical program	9/30/20xx 6/30/20xx 12/31/20xx 12/31/20xx	Task Forces Task Force Task Force CEO – Exec. Committee

Strategy/Initiative

1.1 Develop and implement a firm growth plan for the next five years.
    • Complete and maintain the upside down budget
    • Project internal growth – requires consensus
    • Project growth through acquisition – requires consensus
1.2 Develop a policy and related procedures for capital and debt requirements/limits.
    • Operating capital
    • Admittance of owners
    • Funding of acquisitions
1.3 Manage head count to revenue per FTE in all departments.
    • Establish prior year benchmarks
    • Establish goals for the coming year
    • Utilize outsourcing as appropriate
1.4 Develop a firm marketing and sales plan.
1.5 Develop a training/learning plan.

2.1 Review and update all employment agreements.
2.2 Develop the policy and procedures associated with the election and success of the CEO position.
    • Term of office
    • Re-election policy and procedures
    • Job description
    • Evaluation procedures
2.3 Review and update all stock redemption plans.
2.4 Each employee over age 50 must complete a one-page succession plan.
2.5 Review all insurance policies and evaluate requirements.
2.6 Implement and fund a 401k plan.

3.1 Develop, approve and implement a comprehensive technology plan and three year budget that integrates with the firm's strategic plan.
3.2 Hire a Learning Director to coordinate Continuing Professional Education and technology training.
    • Professional educator with leadership skills
    • Excellent communication skills
3.3 Join the Boomer Circles for coaching, best peer practices and the Extranet.
3.4 Implement a document management system.
3.5 Implement secure client portals with multiple advisor access.
3.6 Implement an integrated financial reporting system.

4.1 Hire a Learning Director.
    • Professional educator
    • Reports directly to CEO
4.2 Complete a training needs assessment.
4.3 Develop a training curriculum.
4.4 Schedule and conduction training sessions.
4.5 Acquire and implement a Learning Management System.
4.6 Implement a centralized help desk and Intranet.

5.1 Review, document and update firm policies and procedures.
    • Internal tax return preparation
    • Sourcing policy and procedures
    • Financial statement preparation
    • Time entry and billing
5.2 Develop a firm sabbatical program.
    • Owners – One month every other year.
    • Principals & managers with over five years – one month every three years
5.3 Implement a balance scorecard plan.
    • Client satisfaction
    • Compliance with firm polices and procedures
    • Financial
    • Training and learning
5.4 Review and update partner compensation plan.

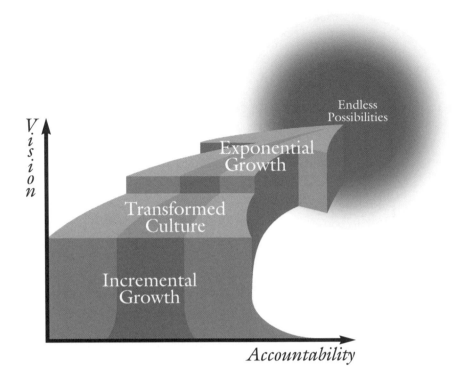

PLANNING × PEOPLE × PROCESS

Exponential Growth
Transformed Culture
Incremental Growth

Chapter 4

CONDUCTING A SUCCESSFUL SUMMIT

No doubt your first question is "why a summit and not a retreat?" "Retreat" gives the connotation of looking to the past and moving backwards. Summit sounds "grander" and, accordingly, should involve a broader base of participants. A Summit is also the beginning of the process that will set your firm apart from the competition. *The purpose of a firm summit is to bring leaders and members together along with outside expertise and facilitation in order to create strategies for improving the firm.*

Most firms spend too little time working *on* the business and too much time working *in* the business. This is especially true in firms where governance is less defined. In those shared services firms, everyone thinks he or she is in charge but is too busy to lead, so little happens that benefits the firm. *Too often firms put the same people in a room year after year and call it a retreat.*

Don't expect exciting and revolutionary results if this is your firm's formula. If you are looking for exponential growth, something has to change. The adage, *"If you always do what you have always done you will continue to get what you have always gotten"* holds true. I can almost guarantee nothing grand will happen unless you change your format, make the meetings fun and create some excitement. Break out of the "professional" mold. If you don't know how, try asking your spouse! The following suggestions will improve the results of your Summit as well as make it an enjoyable experience for all participants.

PLAN TO THINK

Select a relaxing venue away from the office.

Meetings at the office just don't work. They are inefficient, there are too many interruptions and participants have trouble focusing on strategic thoughts. You can't get in the frame of mind for new ideas and change unless you are in a location that takes you out of your daily routine. The best results occur at an out of town location, preferably at a resort with leisure activities to incorporate into daily events. One of the more creative ideas to come about is to conduct the Summit on an overnight sailing trip. If you're not sailors, try a ski lodge or sports arena.

Encourage everyone to participate.

Participation by managers and staff will ensure buy-in — as well as develop new leaders. Fresh ideas and new blood should be welcome. Make the process inclusive rather than exclusive. As I mentioned in the introduction, don't expect different results if you continue using same format. Transportation and lodging expenses are always a consideration, but off-season rates at many venues make them affordable.

Utilize a professional facilitator as your leader.

It is difficult, if not impossible, to facilitate a Summit for your own company or organization. An experienced facilitator will keep participants focused on the agenda. You might be surprised at how focused participants become when an outsider(s) is involved. Selecting a professional facilitator also ensures the Summit will happen as scheduled. Commitment and discipline among all staff members is required in order to ensure success.

Start your Summit with a positive focus exercise.

The positive focus is a powerful exercise that takes only minutes to complete but is generally overlooked by most facilitators. Instead of jumping into the agenda, take a few minutes to reflect on the most positive events that have happened during the past year, why they were important and what, if any, subsequent actions need to be taken. Take time to celebrate and be grateful for your business and personal successes. Doing so will increase the confidence of all participants and will certainly start the meeting on a positive note. Much better decisions are made when participants are confident and positive.

Work from an agenda and stay on time.

Don't surprise participants. Solicit agenda items in advance and distribute an agenda with meeting materials. Do all required homework on agenda items prior to the meeting. Use technology and research staff to get the best information. Keep items strategic and stay on time.

Avoid the numbers, stick to the concepts.

It is too easy for owners and partners to get caught up in the numbers. The tendency is to focus on tactical steps rather than strategic issues. Force participants to think in terms of the *big picture*. Initially tell participants to avoid traditional restraints such as budget and time. It pays to dream. You will always find the time and budget for great ideas and strategies. Chances of identifying great ideas and strategies are diminished greatly if you start with the premise, "we can't afford that." Believe me, any sound business will get to the issues associated with "cost" soon enough in the process. Spend time thinking in terms of who can "pull this off" or "whom do we know that can help us." By staying at the 1,000 foot level, you can see both the business on the ground and the vision in the future.

Keep minutes of the summit and share with the entire firm.

Accountability is critical, and minutes help by documenting assigned responsibilities during the meeting. They are also valuable in avoiding later conflicts and keeping participants focused. They also have value as a reference resource in years to come. Remember the old saying, "What goes around, comes around." Once people have agreed to a course of action, the organization must buy into the vision.

Think strategy rather than tactics.

This is much easier said than done. This is one area where an experienced external facilitator will assist because he or she generally has more control than an internal facilitator. Having an agenda will also help avoid tactical discussions. Its also helpful to remind participants of the benefits of strategic thinking when you announce the dates of your Summit — as well as at the beginning of your first session.

Take 10-15 minutes breaks every hour.

Strategic *thinking* is hard work. Most organizations avoid strategic planning for that reason. People need time to move around and interact in an informal manner. A good rule is to work for 45 minutes and break for 15. This might seem like a lot of "down time," but if you are truly engaged in strategic thinking this time will be spent processing the on going strategic discussions. This will also help you avoid *getting caught up in details.*

Mix in activities such as golf, tennis, or boating.

While social activities require planning and foresight, they should be designed to motivate members of the summit who are more introverted. Team activities such as a scramble in golf are fun and allow those with fewer skills to participate and still enjoy the event. Every firm outing needs a driver for the "beer cart." Just make certain everyone has a role to play.

Invite outsiders, including experts or even clients.

Outside experts and key clients offer a fresh perspective and generally command respect from firm members. While you can't expect them to provide answers to all of your problems, you should expect them to have opinions and ask penetrating questions. Some firms are just learning the benefits of including clients at their annual Summit. Others have been benefiting from the collective wisdom of their centers of influence for years.

Name task forces for follow-up with a responsible person and due dates.

Someone must follow-up and track progress after the decision is made to commit resources to high priority projects. Someone must be in charge and held accountable. Due dates ensure the chances of projects getting completed on time. Allow the responsible party an opportunity to agree upon due dates. This is all part of leveraging your firm's resources. Administrative personnel generally accept responsibility too easily. Learn how to delegate!

Conclude the summit with a brief statement from all participants.

Summits are no different than other business meetings in that people will invariably bring different perspectives. Likewise, people who attend the same meeting often leave with different perceived results. Take time at the end of the Summit to allow all participants an opportunity to voice their perspectives on the most valuable aspects of the meeting and any changes they would like to see in the future.

Create a one-page, laminated game plan.

A one-page, laminated game plan is a proven key to success. Many people have great ideas, but few execute. The one-page, laminated game plan allows you to easily communicate goals within the firm as well as with outside stakeholders. The one-page game plan should include the firm's vision, mission, core values and strategic objectives on side one.

On side two, list the strategic objectives, key measurements, assigned responsiblities and due dates. Lamination is one of the keys to the success of the program. No one throws a laminated document away; they tend to keep it in a convenient location. Review the game plan frequently and hold people accountable.

Top Ten Summit Topics

1. Attraction and Retention of People
2. Governance and Organization
3. Revenue per Full-Time-Equivalent
4. Partner Compensation
5. The Paperless Transaction
6. Outsourcing
7. Developing a Training/Learning Culture
8. Standards, Policies, and Procedures
9. IT Strategies and Budgets
10. Marketing and Sales

Summary Thoughts:

Summits can be fun, productive and thought-provoking. Effective planning, proper facilitation and a pleasant location all contribute to the perceived value of the exercise. Delegate the planning if that's not your unique ability. Every firm has or should have a *social chairman*. Give that person a reasonable budget. Don't wait; schedule your firm's Summit today. You will thank yourself next year and be pleased at the positive results.

Part II

PEOPLE

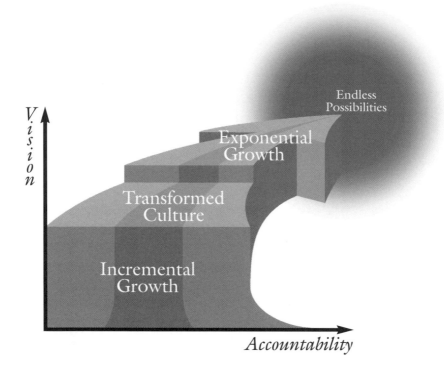

PLANNING × **PEOPLE** × PROCESS

Exponential Growth
Transformed Culture
Incremental Growth

Chapter 5

THE EVOLUTION OF PARTNER VALUE

Partner value and compensation continues to be a hot management topic that attracts considerable attention at firm summits and MAP Conferences. As with all areas of the profession, this issue is being re-evaluated. More and more, the Balanced Scorecard approach — connecting compensation to firm objectives, has emerged within the industry during the past few years.

For the most part, however, individual firms are reluctant to change compensation formulas just for the sake of change. There must be a compelling reason to change — and when it comes to changing the rules governing compensation there are almost always winners and losers. Thus the fear of the unknown is often greater than any motivation for an improved system.

Here are several factors that typically determine a partner's value:

❏ Personal responsibilities
❏ Results over time
❏ Management skills
❏ Client development
❏ Technical expertise
❏ Team focus

The age, size and culture of the firm play a distinct role in its firm's partner compensation plan. The old saying, "be careful about what you measure" is certainly true, and partners are masters at focusing on those things that effect their own compensation.

A common misconception is that a compensation plan is in place for a career rather than for a year or a few years. While I don't imply that firms should change their compensation formulas for the sake of change, it is irresponsible to believe that a firm's initiatives won't change — even if the strategic objectives remain constant for a number of years. The question then arises, "What characteristics are included in a good partner compensation plan and how do firms tend to value partners in today's competitive environment?"

In looking at successful firms, I see seven distinguishing characteristics when it comes to partner valuation. They take into consideration a partner's participation in each area:

1. A current firm strategic plan. (The foundation)

2. Taking time to think and plan. (Working on the firm rather than in the firm)

3. An outside perspective. (Objectivity)

4. A written compensation plan. (Clear and communicated)

5. Communication of that plan "up front." (Fairness)

6. Consideration of each partner's unique abilities. (Performance & job satisfaction)

7. Frequent feedback and communication conducted at least quarterly. (Accountability and coaching)

These seven characteristics can further be broken down into Leadership, Management, Discipline and Accountability. Unfortunately, accountability and discipline are missing today in many firms.

Historically, partners have been evaluated on charge hours, book of business and realization. Older compensation systems tend to focus only on financial results. Newer systems focus not only on the annual financial results, but also on overall staff development (training/learning), client satisfaction and consistent adherence to firm standards, policies and procedures. Also notice that seniority was not mentioned above. Firms should not promote entitlement but rather an environment of accountability with a focus on the firm's strategic objectives.

With that said, the value chain starts at the low end with partners who have technical skills (but not management and client development capabilities) to a high for those partners who are focused on the management of the firm (managing other partners) and client development. In the middle are partners who serve clients, manage non-partner personnel and have limited client development skills or responsibilities. As firms age and grow, they tend to value management skills equally or above mere output. This is often a tough hurdle for many firms to clear because a partner must accept the required changes in both his or her role in the firm and compensation.

In fact, one of the biggest issues with rapid growth and firm mergers is the challenge of getting partners to think like a larger business. To change their thinking we recommend an exercise called *The 10 Times Growth Model*. Force your partners to think. Ask them what the <u>firm</u> would need to do if it was 10 times larger than it is today. After all, our goal in creating this book is to lead firms through the PERFORMANCE³ model in order to achieve exponential growth.

With time, they will arrive at the answers the firm is seeking:

1. A professional management team
2. Quality personnel
3. Increased revenue per FTE
4. A firm managed like a business
5. A training and learning culture
6. Increased capital
7. Documented standards, policies & procedures
8. Development of knowledge management systems
9. Specialization
10. Integrated systems

Consider the contribution to exponential growth each one of these ten factors could bring. But remember, each requires serious thought and a commitment to change.

Next, ask the question what <u>they</u> would need to do if the firm were 10 times larger. Their answers will generally sound like:

1. Become a better manager
2. Adhere to standards, policies & procedures
3. Acquire training & update skills
4. Spend more time selling
5. Form more alliances
6. Delegate
7. Spend less time doing client work
8. Plan more time off
9. Maintain confidence of self & subordinates
10. Upgrade client base

Now for the most important question. Ask them which one of these ten items should be removed if the firm is only growing at 10-15% annually. *The answer is none.* Partners should be thinking like the firm is already 10 times larger than it is today and making decisions based upon the future rather than the past. The firm's growth and profitability must be planned and each partner should be held accountable. There will be disagreement, but that is not reason enough to ignore the important issues. That is firm leadership and management's responsibility.

Change typically is driven by pain, reward and education. In most firms it requires all three, and those that partners respond to most are the pain of change associated with compensation and the reward for doing the *right* things.

Summary Thoughts:

If you are serious about accountability and have a desire to change partner compensation, start with a well defined — strategic plan. As Jim Collins relates about in his best selling book, *Good to Great*, the task of getting the wrong people off the bus may be an easier task than getting the right people in the right seats. Leadership requires tough decisions, and partner valuation requires change, thinking and a sincere focus on written strategies.

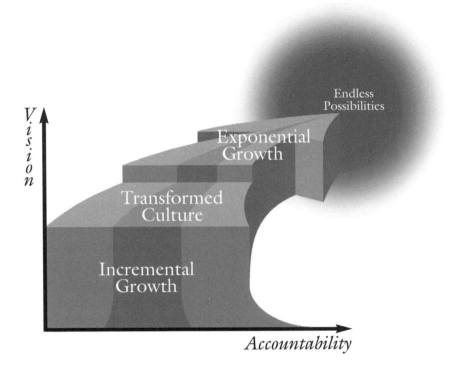

Vision

Endless
Possibilities

Exponential
Growth

Transformed
Culture

Incremental
Growth

Accountability

PLANNING × **PEOPLE** × PROCESS

Exponential Growth
Transformed Culture
Incremental Growth

Chapter 6

BUILDING YOUR TEAM

Human Capital is not just a "buzz word" flying around our industry today. It represents a genuine shift in the mind set of PERFORMANCE³ managers toward how they view the firm's most precious asset — their people. The most progressive firms are finding positive results on the bottom line by "living" the following quote:

"People are *assets* whose *value* can be enhanced *through investment.*"

"As the *value* of people increases, so does the *performance capacity* of the firm."

There are 5 key decisions that firms make to move in this positive and rewarding direction.

Decision #1 - We will develop a "Human Capital" attitude – beginning at the Leadership level:

You have heard it before, and you are going to hear it again – *it is all about leadership.* If firm leadership does not believe its greatest asset is its people, then people will respond (or should I say *not respond*) accordingly. Staff must be recognized as critical to the firm's success. I'm not talking about "fluff" here; I'm talking about cultivating an environment of accountability, teamwork, employee involvement and empowerment. This is achieved by identifying the skills and characteristics needed to make appropriate investments and even tough decisions about letting go of some of your top producers. Ask yourself, are you encouraging the decline of your overall human capital by holding onto staff that resist change, are arrogant, abuse authority, treat staff poorly and don't take the initiative to develop others in the firm just because they are a top revenue producer? If the answer is yes, then it might be time to think about how that one person is affecting the entire team and how letting go of one might produce tremendous benefits.

41

Decision #2 – We will recruit and retain only the best talent:

The first step to retaining employees is to find out why they are leaving! Does your firm have a practice of conducting an exit interview when someone leaves? I suggest that you not only have that conversation, but let an outside human resource professional conduct the interview. This is a prime opportunity for you to learn about your firm and why somebody whats to leave it. You may think it is obvious because they told you they are getting more compensation or have an opportunity for advancement somewhere else.

However, a trained professional will discover some underlying and important reasons that will enlighten and assist you in making changes to retain future employees. In a recent survey, the top 5 *reasons* employee's leave their firm's are:

1) *Lack* of appreciation
2) *Negative* communication of work effort
3) *Lack* of communication about what is happening in the firm
4) *Lack* of help when a problem arises
5) *Lack* of training

Once you discover any necessary changes, the next step is to implement a process to hire talented individuals that fit your culture. This process should mandate seeking staff that fits with three critical areas of success:

Cognative Skills – having the basic knowledge, training and education to complete the tasks that they will be assigned.

Affective Skills – having the motivation and desire to complete the tasks that they will be assigned.

Conative Talent - having the natural instinct to work the way they need to in order to complete the tasks that they will be assigned.

All are important and should be implemented with the process that your firm will use in order to find the most talented individuals to join your team.

Decision #3 – We will communicate effectively with all team members:

Communication is one of the top reasons that employees leave a firm. Your staff wants to know what is going on and how it will impact their jobs. One of the first, and most important, pieces of information you should share is your firm's overall Strategic Plan. Knowing where the firm is going is extremely important to your staff. Don't stop there! The next important step is to show each staff member individually how his or her goals and objectives directly tie to the overall plan for the company. This can be accomplished quickly and easily in the employee evaluation system. Knowing that they are making a direct difference to the overall health and well being of the firm will give them a sense of purpose and show them that they are important and valuable.

Decision #4 – We will hold our team members accountable for results:

I know what you may be thinking. You will scare your staff to pieces if you suddenly tell them you are going to hold them accountable for their goals and objectives. Initially that might be the case. But in the long run, *they will feel more valued as a member of the team if they are given tasks and the expectation is established that they will complete those tasks.* When you link performance to results, the success rates increase dramatically. One word of caution: make the accountably process simple. The act of writing down an action item, steps for achievement, due dates and then — most importantly — talking it through with the team leader is an extremely important process to complete. Remember to listen much and talk little, and give the staff member your undivided attention. He or she must feel more valuable and important than the incoming phone call or the client that is just dropping by.

Decision #5 – We will build a *Spectacular Workplace:*

I am not talking about the way that the building looks aesthetically; I am talking about creating an atmosphere that your staff will brag about! Have you looked at your benefits package lately? Does it include benefits that your staff is hungry for? Have you asked your staff lately what benefits would be valuable to them personally? Is you firm marked with "status distinctions" that show one level of the organization is far more important than others? Have you implemented a training program based on the needs of the staff? Is there a succession plan so the staff knows their future is protected through thoughtful planning? These are just a few of the questions you might ask about your firm. Once again the importance of leadership becomes evident. The really spectacular workplaces today are those that regularly ask these types of questions and then respond as they see the need.

Firms that make the commitment to act on the 5 key decisions described above are those the rest of you will be trying to copy in the near future. They will be the leaders, have the best staff and the wealthiest partner group. They are the ones that "get it" and act on that insight. You decide…The choice is yours!

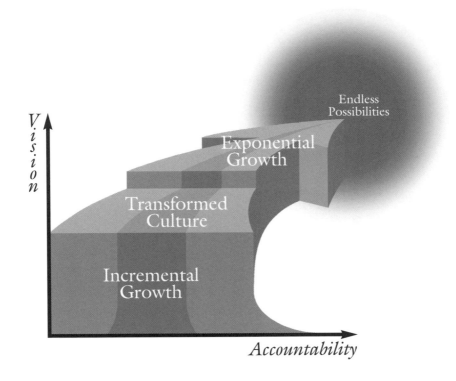

PLANNING × **PEOPLE** × PROCESS

Exponential Growth
Transformed Culture
Incremental Growth

Chapter 7

THE TRAINING/LEARNING CULTURE

Training is one of the most crucial components of any business strategy. It is an excellent tool to recruit the best and brightest employees — and to retain them. Furthermore, it ties directly into your strategy by helping employees increase productivity and develop personally and professionally into future leaders of the firm.

Most business leaders agree that training is important; however, many of those same leaders argue that they can not afford the time commitment to send employees to training. Numbers do not support this argument. Take, for example, the average accounting firm. They average less than 50% chargeable time, which begs the question: What are your people doing with the other half of their time?

Every growth oriented business should commit to training all of its employees. This is especially important when it comes to administrative support and non-technical staff. Your client-facing professionals are not the only employees who will benefit from continuing education. With skilled employees at all levels of your organization, you will become a more efficient and productive firm. Non-accountants are not the only employee segment that is often overlooked. "Soft skill" training is also important to all of your employees. When planning your next round of developmental training, don't overlook such topics as presentation skills, business writing, and team facilitation skills. These courses are often discounted as "non-essential" when, in reality, they teach the skills that speak loudest to your clients about your firm's professionalism.

Building a Training & Learning Culture

The goal of building a Training & Learning Culture is to create an environment in which everyone teaches, everyone learns and each individual focuses on enhancing his or her unique or exceptional abilities.

Achieving this goal starts at the top. Leaders of the firm must commit to developing a Training & Learning Culture. This requires the development of *their own* personal *Teachable Point of View* (TPOV). A TPOV is based upon your ideas and values about training & learning combined with your approach to motivating team members tempered by your ability to make difficult decisions. Leaders should not only be able to put their TPOV's down on paper but should be able to easily articulate them to their firms. A Training & Learning Culture devoted to the development of knowledge has several key benefits to your firm.

Characteristic	Behavior
Develop leaders at every level of the firm	You have capable people at every level of the firm ready to step in and lead a team.
Attract and retain the best and brightest	Intelligent people are always on a quest for knowledge. A culture dedicated to this quest is a magnet to these individuals.
Increase productivity	Skilled workers are always more efficient. Efficiency has a direct impact on your firm's financial performance.
Succession planning through a leader/ teacher pipeline	When adding or replacing partners, you don't have to go outside to look for candidates. You have created qualified successors in your own backyard.

The idea that everybody teaches is important. When people are required to teach, they will inherently want to know the topic inside and out for fear of looking uninformed.

Encouraging people to teach forces them to let down their guards and make themselves vulnerable to peers who may discover what they don't know. Once an individual's guard is let down, the barrier to collaborative learning is removed, and the teacher can focus not only on delivering the knowledge they possess — but also learning from the experiences and knowledge of others.

While vulnerability is typically uncomfortable, a Training & Learning Culture offers significant satisfaction. By opening our minds to others' ideas, we learn new skills and concepts. We also have the satisfaction of watching others develop into tomorrow's leaders before our very eyes. And with a more intelligent and collaborative workforce, we will invariably watch the firm increase its performance.

By contrast, "At Risk Firms" (those that do not commit to a Training & Learning Culture) have several defining characteristics as well.

Characteristic	Behavior
Command and control	Intelligence is based on tenure. "I know more than you because I've been doing it longer."
Cram down attitude	The firm's leaders are set in their ways. Employees will learn and perform consistent with those ways or they can find another job.
Hidden information	Worried about job security, employees hold onto valuable information for fear of making themselves replaceable.
Gamesmanship	A culture of competition. Everyone wants to know more than the others AND prove it.
Leaders learn nothing	"I'm the leader; there is nothing I could possibly learn from these kids fresh out of school." The leader's "superior" knowledge set gets stale and outdated over time, putting the entire firm at risk of falling behind.

Conclusion

All progress starts with the truth! Therefore, you must conduct an accurate assessment of where the firm and its employees are today and where the firm wants to go in the future. Without an analysis it will be difficult for the firm to prioritize initiatives and focus resources to those priorities.

Culture starts at the top of the firm. Without the commitment of the CEO and firm partners it is difficult, if not impossible, to build a Training and Learning Culture. Partners must "talk the talk and walk the walk" to ensure the future success of the firm.

Notes

1 – *Tichy*, Noel with Nancy Cardwell. *The Cycle of Leadership*. New York: HarperCollins, 2002.

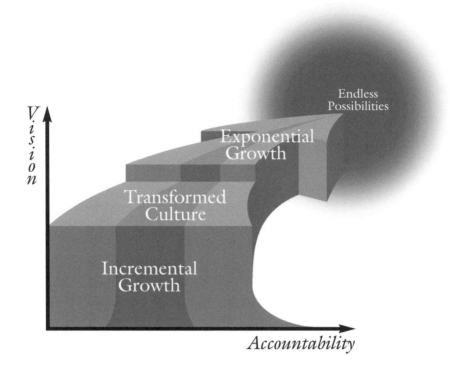

PLANNING × **PEOPLE** × PROCESS

Exponential Growth
Transformed Culture
Incremental Growth

Chapter 8

IDENTIFYING TRANSFORMATION AGENTS

Joseph A. Schumpeter coined the term "creative destruction" in his book *Capitalism, Socialism, and Democracy* published in 1942. Much has been written about it recently due to the fact industry life cycles are becoming shorter. Environments are dynamic, not static, and as a result firms cannot simply focus on "core competencies" as a basis for firm strategy. If they do, they will end up preparing for the past rather than the future. The first thing that some consultants tell firms in a time of decline is to "get back to basics." This sounds like good advice, but is it? During the past five years, the basics in the accounting profession have changed significantly as have the core business services and technology.

The real areas of focus in firms should be on how to transform themselves in order to thrive in an environment of change and uncertainty.

Most partners in firms agree that we are currently in a period of dramatic change; however, few are doing much to change their planning, staffing, vision and values. This statement requires additional comments and examples in order to fully comprehend. Many firms operate well below optimum level due to lack of aggressive leadership, and, in fact, in many cases with leadership that chooses to stick with a strategy of stability rather than being open to adapting to environmental opportunities. When I say exponential level, I am talking about profitability as well as creating an environment to retain and attract top quality personnel. In many cases firms will as, *we have been successful, why change?*

The reasons firms must change are increased competition and complexity. Do you think your firm would be better off if its strategies were fast, creative and aggressive? All firms are in a period of increased competition for quality people and quality clients. Promoting mediocrity is a sure formula for decline and shrinking profits.

Managing an accounting firm in today's environment is not an easy task and is rapidly becoming more difficult. It involves personnel, marketing, innovation, leadership, culture, technology and other areas critical to sustaining long-term success. But there is good news! If you are willing to change your strategies and paradigms, your firm can become more profitable and people will love working there. **Success is a choice as is happiness.**

Assuming your firm makes the choice to be successful, the road will not be easy bacause you will probably have to make significant changes. Those transformations will primarily come in management philosophy. You must be committed to maximizing the future prospects of the firm, staff, owners and clients. The balancing act comes in managing both for today and tomorrow. It is all about your vision. The tendency of accountants is to cut people and expenses at the first signs of reduced profitability. Success belongs to firms and their leaders who capture the future instead of simply waiting for it.

Firm Management must simultaneously manage a three-act play. First, they must maximize current opportunities and existing business (in-the-box thinking). Second, they must lead and encourage others to think and act creatively (out of-the-box thinking). Third, they must allow their people to discover the future (stay ahead of the curve – visionary thinking). Sustaining success is never a result of one component. However, success can be killed by one faulty component, such as a Managing Partner or CEO who is too controlling or out of touch with the future. While they <u>may</u> have been successful in the past, it is going to be increasingly difficult to sustain success in the future if the firm leader doesn't successfully manage all three acts. In order to guarantee this type of leadership, most firms must change their philosophy toward firm management.

In the past, firms have primarily valued the chargeable hour and placed little value on managing the firm. Their tendency has been to under pay for firm management and to over utilize accountants (often owners) in areas such as human resources, marketing, sales and technology.

Let's get back to "creative destruction." The creativity of your competition destroys the value of what you currently do as a firm. This may come about from within the industry or from global forces. It is generally easier to understand a concept when it is outside of your industry or profession. Therefore, let's look at the financial services industry. In recent years they have become commoditized through increased regulation, lower margins and outside competition. (Some of this comes from the accounting industry.) Competition is not a succession of repetitive events, but rather a succession of different events. In today's world of the Internet and globalization, events arrive at an increasing rate of speed. In other words, competition is increasing at a rapid pace. Firms must be prepared to deal with these events rather than simply ignore them. Will your firm be able to compete like its competitors? The answer, of course, will vary upon your size, market and firm life expectancy.

Leadership Development Strategy

First, firm owners must understand if they have a leadership problem. Second, they must develop a strategy to solve the leadership problem if one exists. Consultants frequently get fired when they point out a leadership problem. But under performance on the bottom line is indeed almost always traced to the leadership of the firm. Therefore, **if owners want to increase firm profitability, they must focus on firm leadership rather than on charge hours.** All progress starts with the truth.

Structured for Exponential Growth

Your firm's competitiveness is more relative to your structure and leadership than anything else. The business environment should drive your strategies. This may sound relatively simple, but it isn't because of the complexity of the business environment. Much like an orchestra, everyone in your firm must be in sync in order to make music. The weakest performer can cause a disastrous performance. The same holds for a firm's profitability. Firms fail because they are out-innovated and out-marketed by competitors. Too many firm partners are focused on the past and just trying to "hang-on" until retirement. This is cancerous and will be the death of your firm if it is not aggressively addressed.

15 Strategies for Transformation

Given the business environment, what are the most important business strategies for the future? It is impossible to prescribe without adequate diagnosis, but for the majority of the accounting industry the following transformational strategies are applicable:

1. Select a strong CEO who is focused on the future growth of the firm, its employees and clients.
2. Create a training/learning culture in order to retain and attract the best. Significance is the motivator, not money.
3. Integrity is the foundation of trust for employees and clients. Good people always have great options.
4. Manage the firm as a portfolio instead of a single stock. You must allow for some mistakes.
5. Create the future based upon client dangers and opportunities.
6. Technology is the accelerator that drives the future of the firm and potential for innovation.
7. Eliminate bureaucracy and reduce politics in order to eliminate brain drain.
8. Challenge everything. Nothing is sacred.
9. Develop an intelligence unit (internal & external) that reports to the CEO.
10. Treat your people with respect because that is how they will treat your clients.
11. Keep your firm young. As firms age, they tend to become inflexible and inwardly focused.
12. Great leaders develop successors (at all levels).
13. Develop a future based strategic plan.
14. Measure what is important.
15. Question and re-engineer your processes.

While this list is not all inclusive, it should provide your firm with the basics for improvement and strategies to compete in today's rapidly changing environment. Success is a choice, and it depends upon speed, appropriate risk taking and trust. If your firm doesn't have these characteristics, its future is at risk. If it does, be grateful and support your firm's leadership.

Summary Thoughts:

In his recent blockbuster business book, *Good to Great,* Jim Collins points out that today's successful business operations did not transform over night. It took time, in some cases even decades. The bigger the organization, the longer the transformational time frame. His point is that if you are going to grow exponentially, like all great businesses, you will have to foster a constant state of transformation. If you are not changing and adapting to the market, you cannot grow more than incrementally in today's world.

PERFORMANCE[3] thinking will require every manager and employee to understand the vision clearly, to honestly evaluate his or her place in the firm and to make every effort for excellent performance each day. Without this commitment, exponential growth for individuals and for the firm as a whole will be a significant challenge at best. Collins' point is well received – have a clear vision, hire the best people and develop them constantly, create a plan that is achievable and support your people in their pursuit of goals. Finally, develop best practice processes to support them and watch what happens. **Success is a choice!**

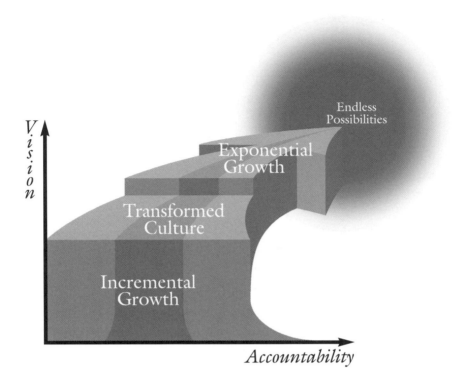

PLANNING × **PEOPLE** × PROCESS

Exponential Growth
Transformed Culture
Incremental Growth

Chapter 9

RETENTION AND ATTRACTION STRATEGIES

Retention and Attraction of good employees has never been more difficult than today. And future indicators suggest little improvement on the horizon. This reality applies to both accounting and technology professionals. Most of us have played that game of "remember when?" Well, let's try our hand at that for a moment.

— Remember when employees were hired right out of college and they looked at employment as a lifetime commitment?

— Remember when you could give a modest yearly raise and tell an employee that he or she was doing a good job, and that person went happily back to work?

— Remember when the market was so full of potential employees that those working for you were just happy to have a job and wouldn't think about looking?

Employees are different now.

— They aren't looking for lifetime employment – they are looking for a potential stepping-stone to a higher-level job.

— Just a yearly evaluation and a raise.

— They know their skills are in demand and there are plenty of employers searching for star performers.

— They also demand more benefits, training and salary. Employers had better be prepared to make adjustments in order to retain the "best of the best." Promotion of mediocrity has too long been an issue within the accounting profession.

In a recent new-student orientation seminar at Kansas State University, participants were told that they would most likely change jobs eight times between the ages of 18 and 32. AMAZING! You might be saying to yourself – "how awful - I would hate to change my job that much." However, this new generation does not see job change as a problem; it is the world they know, and are comfortable with it. We have to find innovative ways to retain employees; and it goes way beyond mere money. What else could it be? Realistically, the list could go on indefinitely. Because of this, your firm has to find ways inovative ways to reach each individual employee. Let's look at a few ideas that have gained popularity in recent years.

Career Development

Employees today are well aware they need to continually update their skills — much more than just 40 hours of continuing professional education. Any more, that's merely the basic requirement for CPAs. What are you doing for those employed in other positions throught the firm? If they see their employer as a hindrance to their ongoing efforts to learn, they will find another that gives them the training opportunities they desire. Employees see great value in a good training plan that allows them to reach their goals. Training is a win-win situation for the employee and the employer. The employee gets to increase his or her knowledge and skills, and the employer has a highly trained and motivated employee working toward the company goals.

Protect the firm — Use an employee contract with a training payout clause in it that applies to specialized training beyond basic CPE. The firm will be investing a lot of money in employee training, and if someone else is going to benefit when the employee leaves, it is only right to expect a payback of a portion of the training expenses. This serves as a deterrent for an employee to leave as well as provides funding for training of a replacement. An example of a training payout clause is:

It is the intention of *Great Company* to invest significantly in professional training and certification for *Star Employee*. If *Star*

Employee terminates his/her employment within a two-year period following completion of professional training or certification, *Star Employee* agrees to reimburse *Great Company* at the following rates for direct training or certification costs, including, by way of example and not limited to, exam fees, certification preparation courses, registration fees, seminar costs and other direct costs related to training: seventy-five percent (75%) of training costs within one (1) year of completion of training and twenty-five percent (25%) of training costs within two (2) years of completion of training.

Job Content

One surefire way to send an employee packing is to give him or her a job that is boring and one that person doesn't enjoy. Make sure, as you structure the position, you give each person duties that will challenge and allow that emplyee to excel. Make sure you do face to face evaluations with your employees at least quarterly to ensure that their job duties are interesting and that the employee understands how his or her job directly impacts the firm.

Protect the firm — Put the job description as well as the quarterly evaluations in writing. Don't leave the expectations of either you or your employee to memory.

Flexibility

Now more than ever, employees want flexibility. We all know that some people are morning people and others don't start functioning until later in the day. Some jobs require an employee to be in the office from 8:00 to 5:00, but others do not. This entire chapter could be devoted to the multitude of preferences employees have for when they work. Don't get caught in the trap of "we have never done that before." Look at each individual situation and make a rational and clear decision — one that will benefit your employee and ultimately your firm.

Protect the firm — Be consistent with your employees. If you are going to allow one employee to work a 10-hour 4-day week, then you must be prepared for the others to ask and expect that you will do the same for them.

Tuition Reimbursement

Higher education is not just a luxury — it is a necessity in many fields. If you have employees looking for the opportunity after college to obtain a higher degree, a tuition reimbursement program may be just the right motivation for them.

Protect the firm — Just like the training programs, you should build a payback clause into the employee agreement; if the employee chooses to leave, he or she will need to payback a portion of the expenses incurred by the firm.

Competitive Salary

A competitive salary relative to you marketplace is essential to keeping a great employee. Although salary is not usually the ONLY reason an employee leaves a company, it certainly plays a part in the decision. If all things are equal, and an employee can make a higher salary somewhere else, you can bet he or she will make the move.

Protect the firm — Do your homework — annually. You can bet your Star Employees will have done theirs. Identify sources that offer good data about comparable positions in your area. Remember to be careful not to compare the positions in your firm only to other accounting firms. Not only are you in competition with other firms — you are in competition with the bank, the technology company and every other business in your community — including your best clients! Remember, this new generation of employee is not affraid of change, and therefore, changing to a new industry is not an issue.

Bonus Plan

Many employees respond well to connecting goals, personal or company, to a bonus plan. Set your company goals, and then set individual goals that will help support the company goals. Next, set the bonus structure to support both personal and company initiatives. Your firm will benefit and so will the employee. Remember, the best thing that can happen to you and your employee is that you will have to pay out on the bonus plan when the company meets its annual goals.

Protect the firm — Put the bonus plan in writing each year. Make sure you stay flexible so that you can change the plan as your firm changes. Communicate very clearly with your employee about what the bonus plan is for, what their roles in obtaining the goals are and how the plan could change from year to year.

Be Creative!

There are as many ways to motivate and retain employees as there are employees that you hire. The better you understand your employees, the better you will be able to offer benefits that motivate them. Some firms have employee parties, set up massages in-house, have contests to give employees chances to win free dinners or gift certificates — the list can go on and on. Find something that will bond the employee to the firm.

In our company, we utilized a creative year-end bonus last year. At the end of our strategic planning session, we met for a year-end celebration and dinner. Between the end of the planning meeting and dinner, each employee had a specified amount to spend on the Internet. There were some rules: 1) Each employee had to spend the money on himself or herself. 2) They had to spend it on the Internet, and 3) They had to be ready to show a picture of what they purchased by dinner. We had a great time doing this and I believe our entire staff has told the story to almost everyone they know. We created a way to build excitement and loyalty among our staff.

Protect the firm — It doesn't matter what you do for your staff, but it is always a good idea to have one person in charge of monitoring all the programs, bonuses and benefits. Don't let individual managers have an open door to making these types of decisions. You don't want some employees getting all the "goodies" while others get nothing. Let one individual in the firm — usually the Human Resources Manager or the Firm Administrator — coordinate these matters.

Ten Tips for Maximum Retention and Attraction

1. Strategic Plan

If your firm does not have a strategic plan, develop one immediately. Without a plan, what do you tell prospective employees about the future direction of the firm? For that matter, what do you tell existing partners and staff? Bright people expect well thought-out strategies and a game plan.

2. Recruiting

Do you know what talent and skills you are looking for? Do you have a job description? Are you using state of the art testing methods such as the Kolbe Index™ in order to attract personnel who meet the job description as well as those who will work well as a team player? Too many firms do not utilize professional human resource people in their recruitment efforts, thus starting the employer/employee relationship in high risk mode.

3. Testing

For the most part the accounting profession hates tests. Most accountants think of testing from a technical perspective. While technical skills are important, they can be taught and learned if you have the right people. Tests such as the Kolbe Index™ present a valuable resource when building a firm that requires teamwork. Too often we see a group of "Mini *Mes*" who are clones of the partner/person responsible for hiring. Kolbe is a *conative* test. The Kolbe Index™ tests for a person's drive and instincts.

4. Training/Learning

Employees today enter the profession expecting to grow through a training/learning experience. All who are at the partner level should be capable and expected to train as well as learn from the experience. Fostering a training/learning environment will differentiate your firm from the competition in today's marketplace.

5. Challenging Experiences

Technology has changed the employee development path in most firms. New employees desire client contact and responsibility — at least the best and brightest do. Much of the training smaller firms provide is on-the-job. Therefore, all jobs and the people responsible for them have an incredible impact upon new employees. If managers and partners are not good leaders *and* managers, they will "turn off" the best and brightest employees.

6. Technology

Bright employees expect state of the art technology and integrated systems. Providing new employees with old technology does not send the right message. The cost of a new notebook computer today is a small price to invest in a valuable employee. It will send a positive message to the new employee as well as increase his or her productivity — provided that person is properly trained.

7. Work - Life Balance

Firms must plan and use better management techniques in order to avoid burning out their employees. A few firms offer 90-day sabbaticals for all partners (every three years) and those who have been in the profession for over five years (30 days). All firms would benefit from such programs as they promote the one-firm concept as well as offer employees a chance to rejuvenate.

8. Hire Non-Accountants

Smaller accounting firms often make the mistake of hiring too many accountants and not enough professional support staff. You don't need to be an accountant to be successful as a training/learning coordinator, human resources professional or an IT specialist. The larger firms have hired non-accountant professionals in both chargeable and non-chargeable roles for years. This relates to the importance of job descriptions and hiring the right people for the job. Unfortunately, smaller firms often utilize accountants in these positions because they are viewed as part-time functions.

9. Manage the Firm as a Corporation

Leadership and governance are both important to retaining and attracting quality personnel. Employees are confused by the partnership form of governance. Employees receive inconsistent and often contradictory communications in the partnership environment. Select a strong CEO and give that person power to lead the firm. With a good strategic plan, firms do not need consensus on every issue in order to effectively and profitably manage the firm.

10. Growth and Marketing

Firms that expect to attract quality employees must be in growth mode. There must be room for advancement, or bright people will not stay with the firm. Turn over is actually good as long as the bottom 10% are leaving each year. Too often the stars leave for better opportunities due to a "log jam" at the top.

Preventing this requires management, goal setting and holding people accountable. Every employee (including partners) should have a 90-day game plan and be held accountable for it. The game plan should focus on four areas: financial performance, training/learning, processes and client satisfaction. This actually takes less time subjectively evaluating personnel during an annual meeting of partners. Immediate feedback is far more effective than an annual review. Performance reviews should not be conducted at the same time as compensation reviews.

Summary Thoughts:

Do you think all of these ideas sound like a lot of work? You bet they are! However, it is worth every bit of the effort you put into it if you can find ways to keep star performers in your firm, performing for you! Remember - your employees reflect your firm, so take the challenge to retain your star performers!

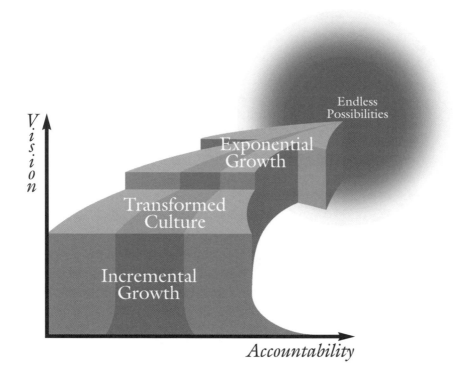

PLANNING × **PEOPLE** × PROCESS

Exponential Growth
Transformed Culture
Incremental Growth

Chapter 10

SELECTING FIRM LEADERS

Many in the accounting profession are experiencing a human resources crisis and a corresponding shortage of future leadership. What are most firms doing about it? Sadly, the problem is not going way. In fact, it will probably increase in intensity. Some firms have implemented leadership development programs in an attempt to focus on the leadership issue.

However, isn't the identification of leaders as important as the development of leaders? I believe that identification is very important and perhaps the most difficult step in the leadership development cycle. When and how do you identify leaders? What do you look for in future firm leaders? What traits do you avoid? Leaders should be identified early in their careers and provided with the opportunities to develop their leadership skills. Potential leaders often leave if they don't have the opportunity to lead and don't see a significant future with the firm. This often occurs when firms stagnate and fail to grow. The following mistakes are easy to make when it comes to leadership.

1. Firms wait too long to identify leaders.
2. Firms focus on consensus building skills rather than leadership skills.
3. Firms hire homogeneous personnel rather than diversity.
4. Firms overvalue problem solvers and fact finding in defining leadership traits.
5. Firms overvalue workaholics. (Charge hours and the effort based economy.)

These issues may not sound that significant, but they are very important in selecting people to lead your firm. Many people think leadership is only necessary at the top of the firm. Leadership is necessary at all levels and good leaders are developed over a career and not in a period of one to two years. Therefore, it is recommended that firms identify leaders as early in their careers as possible and develop an individual professional development plan involving diversified experiences. Good leaders have what Jack Welch refs to as "edge." They can make a decision without every fact. The higher people go in the firm, often the fewer facts they have in order to make a decision. Ambiguity is often present and good leaders must be able to make a decision. Consensus builders tend to wait too long by insuring that everyone is in agreement with the decision. This type of leadership promotes mediocrity.

With this said, what should a firm look for and how can they avoid basing assessment on insufficient information? Knowing what to avoid in identifying and selecting leaders may be as important as a list of criteria.

Awareness of the following should improve your process and help you avoid falling into some common traps.

1. Look for people who have a tolerance for risk.
2. Avoid those who spend too much time in consensus building. (While consensus is important in a professional service organization, it is time consuming and doesn't always lead to good decisions.)
3. Look for those who can manage a diverse group of people. An appreciation of others' unique abilities is the sign of a good leader.
4. Avoid weighing a person's ability to be a good implementer and problem solvers to heavily. These abilities don't necessarily make good leaders. Their tendency is to over analyze and delay making decisions.
5. Look closely at personal integrity and the ability to trust others; this is of utmost importance.
6. Look for the ability to turn dangers into opportunities.
7. Avoid those who are overly competitive and lack humility.
8. Look for those with the ability to engage, inspire and convince others.
9. Identify those who have an instinct to know which problems to solve not just how to solve problems.
10. Look for those that have excellent one-on-one social skills, they are just as important as public speaking.

The identification of leaders is imperative to firm sustainability. Visionary leaders cannot be easily manufactured through leadership development programs. Most good leaders are hard wired and demonstrate their leadership traits in early adulthood. It is your responsibility to look for those traits and nurture them. Future leadership within the firm is attainable at every level of the practice and by focusing on finding the individuals in the firm that value a diverse workforce, have "edge" in their decision making abilities, can make decisions quickly without having all the facts and who have a tolerance for risk, can put your firm in a better position to develop the talent they need for the future. Your firm will then be responsible for developing great leaders through the experiences you have allowed them to engage in. These firm leaders will then chase vision – not just goals!

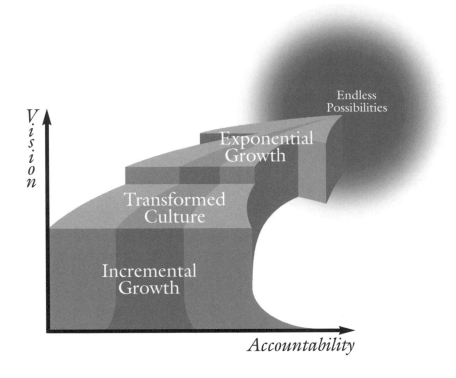

PLANNING × **PEOPLE** × PROCESS

Exponential Growth
Transformed Culture
Incremental Growth

Chapter 11

HOLDING YOUR MANAGING PARTNER ACCOUNTABLE

Managing an accounting firm is not an easy task due to the nature of the ownership and the fact that too often everyone thinks they are in charge; but in reality, no one really has the power and control to lead and manage effectively. The majority of accounting firms have a managing partner in title and responsibility, but often without the authority and power to lead effectively and efficiently. Accountability and discipline are the keys to improving performance and growing the firm. I believe that most people's intentions are good; however, often they get caught in the day-to-day tactical issues and fail to focus on the big picture or strategic goals.

Let's look at the key areas in evaluating your managing partner. The areas should also be part of the managing partner's job description. The primary areas are:

- Leadership
- Management
- Profitability
- Strategic planning
- Team building
- Learning/Training
- Asset protection

Each of these areas is important and worthy of further discussion. The size of your firm, number of partners/owners, and the existing management team will influence the areas of importance. A sample evaluation form might look like this. The following rating scale applies and should be based upon the CEO or MP's job description:

- EE – Exceeds expectations
- ME – Meets expectations
- NI – Needs improvement

Leadership

Criteria	EE	ME	NI
1. Does the managing partner function as the firm's visionary? Does he/she have the proper balance between long-term vision and current results?			
2. Does he/she spend an adequate amount of time thinking about what the firm should look like in three years? Can he/she make a decision promptly & effectively?			
3. Does he/she communicate the vision to all stakeholders? (Partners, staff & clients) Does he/she communicate regularly and consistently? Can the managing partner provide confidence and sustain employee morale?			
4. Does the managing partner participate in associations and attend practice management conferences in order to keep the firm informed of best practices and industry trends?			
5. Is the managing partner visible in the community and does he/she represent the firm well? Is he/she a good role model for members of the firm?			

- EE – Exceeds expectations
- ME – Meets expectations
- NI – Needs improvement

Management

Criteria	EE	ME	NI
6. Does the managing partner function as the firm's Chief Operating Officer? If no, has he/she delegated the responsibility to a qualified person?			
7. Does he/she spend an adequate amount of time holding others accountable?			
8. Are resources allocated in accordance with the firm's strategic plan?			
9. Is he/she enthusiastic and even-tempered?			
10. Does he/she encourage others and build strong teams? Does he/she allow others to receive appropriate recognition?			

Strategic Planning

Criteria	EE	ME	NI
11. Does the firm have a written strategic plan with priority goals, measurements, action steps, assigned parties and due dates? Does the firm's budget properly address the priority goals?			
12. Does the firm have a written marketing plan and budget that integrates with the firm's strategic plan?			
13. Does the firm have a written technology plan and budget that integrates with the firm's strategic plan?			
14. Does the firm have a written human resources (staffing) plan that integrates with the firm's strategic plan? (You must get the right people on the bus, the wrong ones off and everyone in the right seat.)			
15. Does the managing partner involve the right people in the planning process? Can he/she build consensus?			

Team Building

Criteria	EE	ME	NI
16. Has the managing partner empowered a firm management team including administration, marketing, technology, and human resources? Does he hold them accountable?			
17. Does he/she resolve partner conflicts and counsel partners as needed?			
18. Does the managing partner utilize testing such as the Kolbe Index® to build efficient and effective teams?			
19. Does the managing partner limit the number of personnel reporting directly to him? (Generally five or less.)			
20. Does the managing partner enforce the Shared Vision concept, firm standards, policies and procedures?			

Learning/Training Culture

Criteria	EE	ME	NI
21. Does the managing partner support a learning/training culture?			
22. Does he/she require firm personnel to develop a TPOV (teachable point of view) in order to transfer knowledge? (Training and learning is a two-way street.)			
23. Does the managing partner ensure that partners and staff attend learning sessions?			
24. Does the managing partner teach and ensure the firm's culture is consistent among offices?			
25. Does the managing partner continue to learn and grow personally?			

Firm Profitability

Criteria	EE	ME	NI
26. Does the managing partner manage to the strategic plan and budget?			
27. Does he/she require all personnel to develop quarterly game plans? Does he/she hold partner's accountable for their quarterly game plans?			
28. Does the firm have a retirement plan that will ensure the continuation of the firm?			
29. Does the managing partner ensure enforcement of firm policies regarding billings, collections, and partner performance?			
30. Does the managing partner terminate non-performers and those who do not train and develop other personnel?			

Asset Protection

Criteria	EE	ME	NI
31. Does the managing partner keep the shareholder and employment agreements current?			
32. Has the managing partner addressed succession planning? Is there a firm plan in place? Do partners over 50 have individual written plans?			
33. Does he/she regularly review insurance coverage and monitor risk management?			
34. Does the managing partner negotiate and review material legal agreements?			
35. Does the managing partner have a current employment agreement with the firm?			

- EE – Exceeds expectations
- ME – Meets expectations
- NI – Needs improvement

Summary Thoughts:

While these 35 questions are not all inclusive, they should serve a starting point or sample for you to develop your own firm's evaluation form. A significant issue in many firms is the expectation of the managing partner to manage the firm as well as manage a book of business. Many managing partners do not want to give up their book of business due to the fact it is a security blanket as well as the fact they like dealing with clients. In larger firms, the firm is best served if the managing partner transfers his/her book of business to other partners and focuses on firm business. An employment agreement for a fixed term of years (generally 3-5 year term) is appropriate. If the partners decide to vote the managing partner out, he/she has a "golden parachute." Likewise the managing partner should expect to inform the other partners at least one year in advance of retirement or if he/she intends to relinquish the role of managing partner.

As important as defining what you expect your managing partner to do is documenting what you believe he/she should not be doing. A simple question like "what are the three things the managing partner should stop doing" is as relevant as any of the above 35 questions. Leadership and management skills are different and often confused by the partner group. It is difficult for one person to focus on both vision and goals. Therefore, it is recommended the managing partner develop a management team building off his/her unique abilities.

Hopefully this will get your firm thinking and acting on formalizing the process of professionally managing your firm. This is advice you would give your clients. Apply it in your own firm and experience improved performance and teamwork.

Part III

PROCESSES

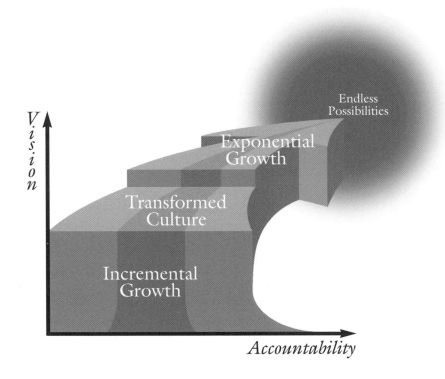

PLANNING × PEOPLE × **PROCESS**

Exponential Growth
Transformed Culture
Incremental Growth

Chapter 12

IMPROVE PROCESSES AND PROFITS

When you start to talk about process, those who have had Business Management 101 immediately think of Frederick Taylor and his time and motion studies. Resistance often follows and professionals say, "I don't want to work in an assembly or production line." Before we give up, let's first define process. ***A process is an organized group of related activities that together create value to clients.*** No single task creates the desired value. Value is created by the entire process in which all tasks are merged in a systematic way for a clear purpose. Without processes, firms crumble in chaos and conflict. Every firm has processes; but are the processes as efficient as they should be? More importantly, have they changed over the years to reflect the changes in technology and client demands? I don't believe they have changed significantly enough in most firms for a variety of reasons, with resistance to change being a primary reason.

Do you know that your clients don't care anything about your processes? They only care about results and processes are what create the results that you deliver to your clients. Some of you have perhaps already read enough. If the clients don't care about our processes then why should we spend any time worrying about processes?

Clients, results and processes cannot be separated. They are like a triangle. There is a very good chance your firm is caught in a trap where no one is focusing on all of the steps it takes to create value. Instead, the work that creates results is broken into pieces and across various departments such as tax, audit and client services. Staff and managers tend to focus on each of the steps that lead to value creation in their department, but no one focuses on all the steps together as a unit or a process. When this happens, there is redundancy, inefficiency and personnel do not function consistently as a team. In fact they often compete and work against each other. Many firms are starting to figure out the value of processes and improving some of their basic processes such as tax return preparation and the preparation of financial states.

Activities in a process are related and organized. Processes are designed to do the right things in the right order all of the time. Typically accountants like checklists. Processes are not done just to keep busy, but rather to create results than clients care about. Too often individuals are focused too narrowly on their tasks and are not aligned toward a common purpose. Therefore, the consistency necessary to reduce time, improve quality and improve client satisfaction is not present. This can all be done with process improvement, but I must caution you that it isn't easy and you will probably experience resistance from existing managers and partners. Many don't want to give up their individual power in order to improve the entire firm. Others are just concerned about change and particularly changing the environment within the firm. Someone must be responsible for a process for it to succeed. Being responsible includes the design, installing, training and ensuring that the process is adhered to. You can also expect the process to be dynamic. It should continue to change with new technologies, regulations and client requirements. Remember that process improvement is about progress and not perfection.

Ask yourself a couple of questions about your firm. Is your firm organized? Is it together? Being organized requires discipline. To be organized, you must have specific processes so that performance isn't determined by improvisation or luck. Being together requires teamwork. It also means you must create the environment in which all staff are aligned around common goals and see themselves as team members rather than as adversaries. Most firms have some degree of organization and claim they work as a team. But, are they as disciplined as they will need to be for the future and do their teams have the right game plan? By now, some of you are thinking that you have been very successful operating the way you have and are asking, "Why do we need to change?" Simply stated, the answer is that the past is the past and now is now. For the most part, clients had nowhere else to go. They didn't have the Internet and frankly were not as informed as they are today. Compliance services are becoming a commodity and firm's must differentiate themselves or be caught in a great price war. Those that differentiate and relate to their clients will be rewarded nicely.

The good news is that remarkable improvements are typical. Firms that improve their processes see significant reductions in time, improved quality and reduction in costs that relate to increased profitability. To date, most of the success stories have been outside the accounting industry, however, many firms are trying to improve their processes in the tax and audit area. Those that have taken on the challenge and committed to the process have experienced significant improvements. They will also be the first to tell you that it hasn't been easy. Often there is some blood shed, especially within the partner group. I recently heard a great story about a top 100 firm that instituted process improvement in the tax preparation area. The results have been very positive, however, they did have to implement a policy that everyone must comply with the process unless they were within 6 months of retirement and had a retirement date in writing.

It is possible to succeed, but most firms go about changing their processes in a way that is destined to fail. ***The tendency is to experiment rather than commit.*** While this may have been appropriate thinking twenty years ago, it doesn't work today. A halfhearted attempt is not good enough. Changing compensation is generally necessary to change behavior. You should consider changing your compensation plan to a performance based plan. A plan based upon experience and charge hours probably isn't representative of the behavior you are trying to foster in today's process based firm. The compensation formula should measure three performance factors: process, personal and firm performance. The benefit of this type of system is that it rewards personnel for creating client value, not just keeping busy. It also fosters teamwork and reminds employees there are no winners on a losing team. Expect resistance to any change in the compensation system. Also expect the elimination of functional silos in the firm. Everyone will become more focused on the client.

Another advantage of processes is that they tend to reduce the need for management personnel as compared to traditional firms. Employees require less management and managements' focus is on the process rather than the supervision of people. Most of the resistance will come from the management ranks as their jobs are changing. They are now focused on enabling personnel to succeed rather than managing them so they don't fail. Technology plays an important roll by allowing firms and their clients to succeed today as their systems become more client centric rather than application centric. Those clients who have installed ERP (Enterprise Resource Planning) systems are probably ahead of most accounting firms. An ERP system requires discipline and teamwork...organized and together. Those who have implemented an ERP system for a client know that the technology is the easy part. The culture and people problems are far more difficult to deal with.

The last and perhaps one of the most important advantages of process improvement is from the marketing perspective. Let me explain the concept by asking a few questions:

- Do you and your employees have difficulty communicating our services to clients?
- Do you agree that many services are becoming commodities?
- Does your firm have fixed fee engagements?

The answer is probably "yes" to all of these questions. By defining processes you not only make them more efficient, but you can also make them easier to understand and sell. A unique name and a definitive statement that is consistently communicated by everyone in the firm will go a long way in improving communications as well as sales. Others in the financial services arena have been doing this for years. Every firm I know of has had a client tell them they didn't know the firm did that kind of work and has purchased a service from someone else who did a better job of communicating and selling their services. A few quick steps to process success are:

1. Define the steps in your processes. Eliminate those that are redundant or don't add value.
2. Name the process.
3. Develop a graphic for each process showing the major steps.
4. Prepare a definitive statement (concise and consistent) about your processes for use by everyone in your firm.
5. Train all personnel.

Processes require leadership, change in thinking and a change in firm culture. Financial services and other service companies are followers compared to the manufacturing industry when it comes to processes. The cultural shifts associated with processes are:

- From individual to team
- From lack of responsibility to accountability
- From boss to client
- From improvisation to discipline
- From conflict to sharing
- From effort to results

These are difficult changes for some people to accept, but necessary for firms to continue to compete and provide clients with value. Remember that client value comes from leadership (direction), relationships (confidence) and creativity (new capabilities). Improved processes will allow you and your firm to provide greater value in a reduced amount of time.

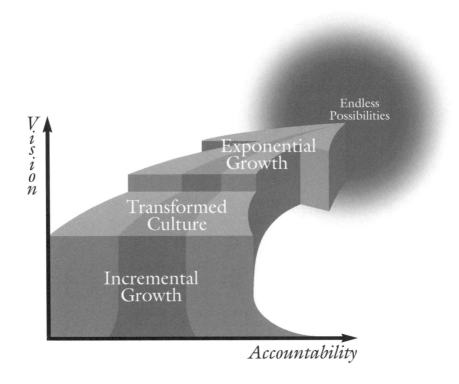

PLANNING × PEOPLE × PROCESS

Exponential Growth
Transformed Culture
Incremental Growth

Chapter 13

GLOBALIZATION —
THE IMPACT ON PROCESSES

Much has been written on outsourcing and its impact on the accounting profession. While everyone has their opinions and beliefs, it is time for all firms to seriously evaluate strategic options that will help transform their service offerings and business model. These strategies should allow firms and partners to take advantage of technology and other resources. Solutions to the issues facing their small and medium business clients and their owners should be the primary focus. The services and technical skills that most firms have delivered over the past 20 years are either becoming obsolete or commoditized with shrinking margins. If you don't believe this, take some time and think before you answer the following questions:

1. Can someone else provide the service cheaper? (It doesn't matter where in the world they are located.)
2. Can technology improve your processes, quality and speed?
3. Are the services we offer satisfying the requirements of our clients?

The initial tendency is to be defensive and say "we are meeting the needs of our clients in an efficient and professional manner. We just completed our best year financially." But, are we as a profession really meeting the needs of our clients? Have our clients' needs changed? Are firm's positioned for the future? In the past, clients were reasonably happy with CPAs offering tax and accounting services. Today, clients demand services that are broader based and require accountants who see the "big picture" rather than simply offering specialized skills. Don't discount the value of specialization, but think more about the demand for the person that can manage relationships and integrate various solutions. Again, the tendency of most CPAs is to gravitate back to increased technical skills versus relationship skills. Daniel Pink in his recently published book *A Whole New Mind* stresses we are moving from the "information age" to the "conceptual age". Knowledge workers were the core of the information age while creators and empathizers will be the core of the conceptual age.

A good example of what I am talking about is in the area of tax planning and research. Skilled researchers who utilize technology will be most effective if they have relationship skills rather than just technical skills. Technology and globalization will impact the services, while the value from the relationship will grow if the accountant can assist the client in identifying requirements and providing world class solutions internally and through alliances.

Most firms are starting to think differently due to the lack of qualified personnel and client requests for non traditional services. The challenge is to get partners and experienced personnel to change during a period of prosperity. Change typically does not occur without the threat of loss or the potential for a great reward. In my opinion, we are at that point and firms must make the decision of excellence or mediocrity. The risk increases when firms resist changing processes and utilizing new technology to improve service and reduce time requirements. Specific examples of industry transformation are:

1. Workflow systems that allow projects to be assigned tracked and completed with a reduced amount of partner and review time. Tax returns and other projects can be transferred among firm employees, offices or sourced. Some of the companies that have been pioneers in this area are SurePrep, Datamatics, MphasiS, Xpitax (XCM) and CCH. These applications will only improve and all are written in a web-based environment. This is about process improvement and reduced cycle time. Globalization is not just about "cheap labor." Many industries are breaking large projects into small pieces and sourcing them around the world or even to other offices. You may ask why? Because they can due to the capabilities of the internet. Accounting is not the only profession facing a labor shortage in the United States. The legal profession is the exception. There are still too many lawyers. Architects, engineers, medical and the sciences all are facing shortages, including academics. Workflow allows firms to do more with fewer people.

2. Digital content management systems have grown from the paperless initiative, document management, records management, and email management. There are significant challenges that firms must overcome with regard to compliance and changing outdated processes. However, the rewards and improved client service are significant. Digital content management is also part of workflow and improved processes. With a great system, firms can manage versions, control access and properly destroy records in accordance with regulations and firm policies.

3. Portals are the future platform for delivery of services to clients. This secure environment will provide clients access to documents 24/7. Some refer to this as the "self service" model. Clients will enter or allow the portal to aggregate information digitally rather than in a paper format. The financial services and legal industries are already offering these types of services. The excuse that clients aren't asking for portals can only be addressed by the fact it is what you don't know you don't know that costs you a lot of money. Firms that are using portals report clients love them once they understand the capabilities. The big decision for service professionals is who will control the portal? Whoever controls the portal naturally becomes the primary business advisor. CPAs are currently the most trusted business advisor, but will they take the lead and offer clients this new capability? Once clients start using a portal, they will want all of their documents accessible from the portal (i.e. tax returns, financial statements, broker statements, medical records and legal documents such as leases, wills and trusts.)

4. Future hires should have different skills sets than in the past. Many universities are not changing their curriculum fast enough to address globalization and the capabilities of technology. In fact, firms should look at business majors and management information systems candidates who have better IT skills and a broader based business education. Training and learning coordinators from leading US firms report the training time required for personnel with IT background and database knowledge is much less than for those employees with a traditional accounting degrees. Sourcing companies in India spend more time training personnel than firms in the United States. It is not uncommon for sourcing companies to provide employees 100-150 hours of training before every preparing a tax return. In the United States, it is often on-the job training. Technology also can be utilized to monitor errors and determine additional training requirements. This is part of increased accountability and improved processes.

5. Training and learning are critical to the retention and attraction of quality personnel. Partners are not exempt from utilizing the tax, accounting, practice management, email and content management systems that are affordable and available today. Attitude toward systems and teams are of utmost importance. Rugged individualists will not win in the global economy. According to the Garner Group, five hours of capacity are obtained from every hour of training. Training reduces mistakes, wasted time figuring out how things work, and re-doing bad work. Great organizations that are capable of competing in the global economy have developed training/learning cultures were it is a two-way street. Everyone learns and everyone is expected to train others. Training and learning organizations do not of succession and leadership issues. Great leaders develop their successors.

Firms should not wait. They should develop alliances and relationships with sourcing companies as well as review their hiring strategies and standards. Don't be afraid to ask for help; you can get there much quicker and avoid many of the risks. The firms who ignore globalization and the current personnel challenges will struggle while those who adapt and transform will move to higher levels of service and reduce the impact of commoditization. Think in terms of your *current firm* and your *future firm*. The current firm must provide the cash flow for the future firm. How will your firm look in three years? What new services will you offer? What new alliances will you have? How many of your partners will retire? Peril or promise? The choice is yours and will be determined by your strategic plan and how well you execute. Simply focusing on charge hours will not be enough.

Unique processes are key to organizational efficiency and the ability to train others. Smaller professional service firms tend to have multiple processes while larger organizations transform to the firm's unique process. In fact many smaller firms often act more like sole proprietorships sharing overhead rather than as a shared vision firm. Globalization has allowed firms to think about processes such as:

- ❏ Tax return preparation
- ❏ Billing and collections
- ❏ Financial reporting

Firms should ask some basic questions and review their existing processes. We suggest utilizing block diagrams in order to evaluate existing processes. Some of the review questions are:

- ❏ Do we have redundant steps in our process?
- ❏ Are we utilizing technology to maximize efficiency?
- ❏ Is sourcing a viable alternative for any or all steps in the process?
- ❏ Do we have written standards, policies and procedures?
- ❏ Is everyone (at all levels within the firm) adhering to the standards, policies and procedures (accountability)?
- ❏ Who is responsible for enforcement?
- ❏ Will this process still be viable in three years?

Companies have many processes and most can be improved; but to do so requires innovation and an attitude of continual improvement. Another often forgotten step in process improvement is the naming of the processes. By naming processes, you own the process. And when you own the process, you instantly become more competitive in a commoditized market. Improved processes and workflow will make your firm competitive both locally and in the global economy. Technology is rapidly leveling the playing field from a global perspective.

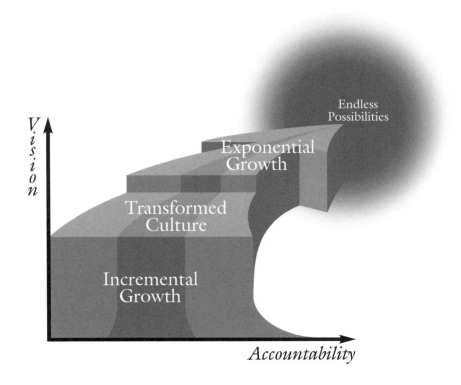

PLANNING × PEOPLE × **PROCESS**

Exponential Growth
Transformed Culture
Incremental Growth

Chapter 14

THE CHALLENGES OF DIGITAL CONTENT MANAGEMENT

Firms are investing heavily in digital document management believing they will receive a significant return on their investment. Some are going to be disappointed and frustrated because they did not do enough thinking and planning up front. Don't misunderstand; the investment is necessary and the benefits are huge if your firm approaches the project properly. Electronic documents are growing exponentially in firms because the technology is affordable and relatively easy to use. Keep in mind, however, that automation does not fix bad processes and procedures. Therefore, firms should evaluate their objectives as well as assess risks when implementing new systems. This cannot be viewed as a "clerical" function and delegated to a lower level within the firm. The vision should start at the top. After all, responsibility to provide the planning security and implementation (from a legal standpoint) stays with senior management.

First the process was called paperless, and then document management and now content management. Let's expand the definition of content management to include all corporate documents and email, records and even, knowledge management. Coupled with knowledge management are client portals or secure digital storage environments that clients can access via the Internet. The digital storage world has evolved significantly over the past ten years and email is now one of the biggest issues when managing content. There are issues and problems associated with any technology project, but these seem to be more significant with content management projects if you haven't spent time planning and thinking before purchasing hardware and software.

Many partners have been led to believe this is a technology project and IT people will take care of the issues. Wrong! **This is a firm project that requires planning by a sophisticated team with expertise and influence.** The team should be comprised of:

- ❏ Management – someone who has the authority and ability to allocated resources.
- ❏ Records management – someone who has knowledge of current processes and procedures as well as the know-how to develop written policies and procedures.
- ❏ Legal – counsel who specializes in records retention and the potential liability of capturing, storing and retrieving content. (This is particularly important with regard to assurance services and email.)
- ❏ Information technology – personnel with knowledge of systems, storage capabilities, retrieval and security of content.

This may sound like a high-level, firm-wide task force, and it needs to be. Too many firms have delegated or relegated content management projects to administration, information technology or other departments rather than enterprise leaders and consultants.

You may feel immune to these issues because you either don't do any auditing or don't audit public companies. I encourage you to think about your responsibilities regarding content in email and if you have the proper policies and procedures in place to protect the firm. Has everyone in the firm been trained about those policies and procedures? Are they being adhered to by everyone? What about spoliation? Under the law, it means intentional alteration or destruction of a document. Do you have policies in place to prevent this from happening in inappropriate ways? And, just in case I haven't gotten your attention: Do you have a written policy on pornography? What happens if one of your employees downloads pornographic material at the office or home using an Internet connection and or computer supplied by the firm? It is your responsibility to have a policy in place and to enforce that policy. Courts may interpret the law to hold the firm as well as the employee responsible, especially if the firm has been negligent with its policies and training.

Content management encompasses a great deal. The following list summarizes some necessary requirements to implement a successful digital content management system. It is more than a hardware/software or IT project.

Some of the most important considerations are:

1. Planning and thinking
2. Written policies and procedures
3. Compliance with those policies and procedures
4. Commitment of senior management
5. Flexibility
6. Commitment of resources (dollars, time and people)
7. Education of all employees
8. A team approach to planning and implementation
9. Rapid response when issues arise (during and after implementation)
10. Centralization and standardization (policies and procedures must be administered consistently throughout the firm.)

In the near future, you will be faced with decisions regarding retention, version controls and security. Are you prepared? Do your policies and procedures address these issues? Why are they important? Can't you just save everything because disk space is so cheap? The answer is a qualified "maybe."

There are several factors to consider:

1. Assurance services requirements.
2. Pending or potential litigation.
3. Security and management capabilities.

There are many opinions and multiple philosophies, but few firms are tested unless they are involved in litigation. Those that have been involved in litigation typically believe that "less is better" if your policies support the clean up of audit files and email. Rules currently apply to public company audit files, and those rules are likely to "trickle down" in many or all states to private and not for profit companies. There are also firms that take the approach used in the broker/dealer business and they save everything. The technology is available and affordable to do so. Here's the catch; if you are faced with litigation, it will be expensive to defend yourself due to the pure volume of records legal counsel will need to examine.

One strategy for email is to give users 90 days to file important messages and documents. At the end of the 90 day period, the system automatically deletes any remaining documents. This rightfully places the responsibility on end users. It requires a written policy, procedures for guidance and training. Bear in mind however, that leaders are ultimately responsible for ensuring people comply with published policies and guidelines.

Another concern is the use of portable document format (PDF) files. They are similar in some ways to paper files in that they do not contain all of the meta data as a file produced by tax software or in an email message. It is too early to know how courts will rule with respect to these files. Firms should also be concerned about the responsibilities assumed in acquisitions when the acquiring firm uses different applications than the acquired firm. You may be responsible to retain any software in order to read and produce files that are obsolete. A strategy to convert email files to the firm standard is recommended.

By now you should realize that the more you know — the more complicated and comprehensive content management becomes. It requires discipline and consistency when enforcing policies and procedures. Attorneys with whom I have spoken believe it is of utmost importance to adhere to and enforce policies. Not having any policies can be viewed as negligence.

These concerns are real and point to the importance of risk management. Therefore, it is imperative to involve experienced legal counsel, records management expertise, technology personnel and high level management in the planning and implementation of a content management system. Deferring the decision-making process (ignoring the risk) is not a good decision. Thinking and planning will save a significant amount of time in the future as well as reduce the firm's risk.

You should consider the following steps to better manage you risk, even if you currently have a "paperless" or document management project in progress.

- ❏ Identify members of your Content Management Committee
- ❏ Review and confirm your objectives
- ❏ Develop a Content Management Transition Plan for communication and accountability

These three critical steps will get you on the right track toward reaching your goals.

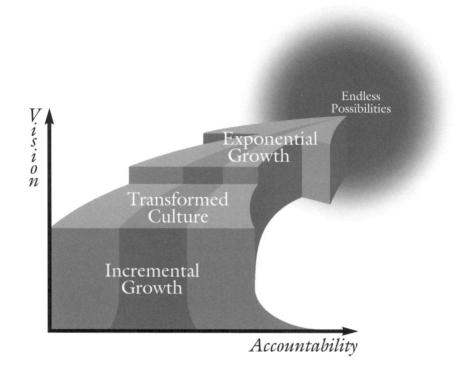

PLANNING × PEOPLE × PROCESS

Exponential Growth
Transformed Culture
Incremental Growth

Chapter 15

IT GOVERNANCE, FOCUS AND EVALUATION

❑ Who is in responsible for IT in your firm?
❑ Do you have a written technology plan and budget?
❑ Is technology viewed as a strategic asset or overhead?
❑ Are you adequately staffed in the IT department? In the firm?
❑ Do you have the right people on your IT Team?

These are all important questions and your firm should be able to provide definitive answers if you expect to compete in a rapidly changing digital and global economy. Many traditional services are being commoditized and profit margins are pressured. With the right technology you can compete as well as offer new higher value services.

The good news is better software, integration and web related tools are available and more are on the horizon as bandwidth increases and becomes more accessible. The demand for IT services is being driven by what end users can do at home rather than what they can do at the office. Granted, core applications such as tax return preparation, financial reporting and time and billing are still important. However, Google, Microsoft and the Internet now define the capabilities desired by end users such as search, access and integration of applications. *Vision, leadership and implementation skills are all necessary in an accounting firm and frankly the IT skills of the average partner and accountant are below where they need to be in order to remain competitive.* A good training program will do wonders for your productivity.

People and growth in revenue are generally mentioned as the top priorities in firms while infrastructure and technology are seldom viewed as critical components in providing the firm with capacity and capability. Firms continue to spend 5-7% of net revenues on technology, but are they getting the return on investment they should? Are they investing in the right things? Sadly, the majority of firms continue to invest in the same core technologies they have invested in for the past 5-10 years. They should be spending more of their technology investment on new technologies and training. Gartner consistently states that for every hour end users spend in training, they increase their capacity by five hours. Training also reduces frustration and increases confidence.

What are the new technologies that firm's should be investing in? Here are a few good examples:

1. Digital content management (Firms should be in compliance with NASBA, AICPA, SEC, State and Sedona Guidelines.)
2. Search, version control and check-in/out capabilities
3. Web access and the ability to work remotely
4. Portals (Service centers on the web for clients, advisors and service teams.)
5. Data extraction and analysis
6. Integration
7. Security and privacy

These technologies require planning, people and processes plus **"change management."** Processes and policies should change in order to leverage the capabilities of the technology. Success requires more than technical skills in moving a firm forward. IT leadership requires the following skills:

❏ Communication and marketing
❏ Project management
❏ Budgeting and cash flow
❏ Human resources
❏ Business savvy
❏ Technical

One person generally does not have all of these skills; therefore, either an internal IT Team or sourcing is required. *Another flaw in firm thinking often is these are IT projects. They are firm projects and should be lead by firm leaders with IT support.* Good examples are integrated financial reporting and content management. The IT leader (CIO – Chief Integration Officer) should have a job description and be evaluated on different performance criteria than your typical manager or partner. The following is a sample list of key functions this leader should be responsible for:

1. Provide IT leadership and vision.
2. Serve on the firm's management Team.
3. Develop, manage and implement the firm's technology plan.
4. Serve as a member of the firm's technology committee.
5. Identify and direct the necessary task forces for high priority initiates (i.e. document management, training/learning, and standards, policies and procedures).
6. Design and implement facilities in order to provide secure systems.
7. Insure compliance with software licensing agreements.
8. Manage and staff a centralized "help desk" for IT support.
9. Provide resources to the firm's Learning/Training Coordinator.
10. Network with industry leaders and attend IT related meetings with the IT leadership of peer firms.
11. Provide required IT resources to various departments/entities of the firm.
12. Manage the development of a business continuation plan and on-going compliance. (Systems documentation and backup procedures are integral parts of the overall plan.)
13. Schedule and conduct Technology Team meetings and the annual technology retreat.
14. Identify and manage testing of new technology.
15. Communicate the firm's IT strategy through the use of a one-page laminated IT plan.

The evaluation of IT personnel should be consistent with their job descriptions and focus on priorities in four areas. They should be consistent with a balanced score card approach.

Financial	Managing to a strategic technology plan and budget.
Learning/training	Continued growth in skills, certifications and development of others.
Standards, policies and procedures	Adoption and adherence to operating polices and procedures.
End User Satisfaction	Based upon end user surveys.

The other focus of evaluations should be on how the person adds value to the firm. While value may be subjective to some, there are three basic characteristics in adding value (internal or external). They are:

Leadership	Provides direction
Relationship	Provides confidence
Creativity	Provides new capabilities

Evaluation criteria alone are not enough. Many firms attempt to start the evaluation process without a basic foundation. A written strategic plan built upon a clear vision, mission, core values and prioritized strategic objectives will dramatically increase the chance of firm and employee success. Getting the right person in the right job is the key. Job descriptions will greatly increase the success of the employee and the satisfaction of the firm. It is difficult to clearly define the job without a strategic game plan. This is especially true in jobs that are not front stage production jobs. Back stage jobs require thought, planning and must be directly related to the strategic objectives of the firm.

Many firms utilize technology teams or committees. Size of the firm and the capabilities of the IT leaders determine the nature of these groups. In some firms these committees are simply used as a communication channel and for gathering end-user input. In other firms they act as the IT governing body and are responsible for planning, staffing and the IT budget. Warning...don't put all researchers on the committee or you may end up doing significant research, but unable to make and decisions and move forward. Task Forces can also be employed for individual objectives or projects. The frequency of meetings and time commitments are determined by the firm's requirements and size of their support staff. Active committees tend to create a sense of confidence within the firm and insure priorities are addressed.

In conclusion, IT Governance is much like firm management. It can be a thankless job, but should be strategic and provide the firm a competitive advantage. If Technology is strategic in your firm, you will be able to attract and retain quality people. If not, prepare for the same IT staffing challenges as you are now experiencing with accountants (entry level and experienced). The choice is yours. Think, plan and grow.

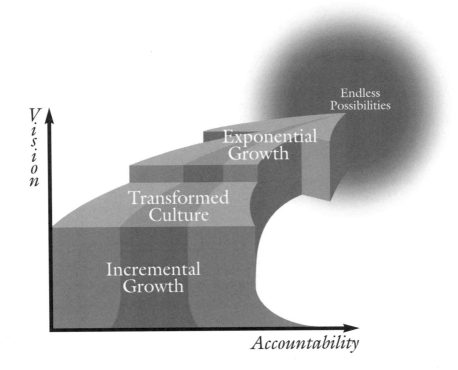

PLANNING × PEOPLE × **PROCESS**

Exponential Growth
Transformed Culture
Incremental Growth

Chapter 16

PRESCRIPTION FOR THE PROFESSION

AICPA chair Leslie Murphy in her recent address to Council stated "one out of six CPAs left their firms during 2004." The cost to replace these people is estimated at 1.5 times their current salary. Enrollment and graduation are up in accounting programs according to the most recent statistics published by the AICPA. The bad news is that the percentage of graduates going into public accounting has dropped to 29% of the total. When speaking with CPA partners I typically ask the question: do you have or have you recommended public accounting to a son or daughter? 95% generally look at me and either say or demonstrate body language that indicates their children would not think of going into the profession. In fact, they often make comments like "my kids don't want to work the hours or do that kind of work." If that is true, how do they expect to recruit their neighbors' children? Things must change and many partners know it. They simply choose to immerse themselves into solving client problems and focus on charge hours hoping the problem is short term and will go away.

More bad news is that staffing is not a short-term problem in the United States. Demographics show the workforce will be short on skilled workers and many in the accounting profession are reaching retirement age. In fact, we often hear the question: "who is going to buy me out?" That is a good question and one that many in the profession have waited too long to ask and resolve. The sign of a great leader is they also select and develop their successor. In the accounting profession the tendency in many firms had been to focus on charge hours rather than the development of leaders at all levels in the firm. All progress starts with the truth and it is time for many in the profession to address the fact they will be leaving over the next ten years. Firms are going to have to do more with fewer people. Planning, people and processes will be the keys to success. Technology will be the accelerator. In fact, many firms are starting to reward people for recruiting, developing and managing others and not just for managing a book of business.

First, let's quickly examine how many firms got into the position they are in today. While it is tough to generalize, the following factors have contributed too many firms' current situation.

1. Lack of a shared vision and strong leadership.
2. Governance by committee or partners rather than a CEO of MP.
3. Lack of a training/learning culture where learning is a two-way street.
4. Focus on charge hours for billing and pricing services (effort versus results based economy).
5. Lack of the necessary growth to attract and retain top quality people.
6. Lack of firm standards, policies and procedures (shared overhead versus shared vision).
7. Lack of accountability at the partner level.
8. Perception that technology is overhead rather than a strategic asset.
9. Commoditization of traditional services.
10. Increased regulation and litigation.

This can either be a list that will prompt you into action to transform your practice or you can choose to ignore the warning signs until it is too late to respond. Firms that do act can quickly transform their firm into emerging and growing markets. In order to do so, they must build consensus among their partners or even terminate some partners in order to make the decisions necessary to enable them to attract quality employees and clients. Some of those changes in attitudes are as follows:

From:	To:
Multiple visions	Shared vision
Billing by the hour	Billing for value
Required CPE	Training/learning culture
Little value on management	Great value on thinking, planning and growth
Mediocrity in personnel	Quality professionals in all positions
Effort based economy	Results based economy
Managing a book of business	Managing and developing people
Commoditization	Unique processes

While this sounds simple, most people do not change for the sake of changing. They typically change due to fear or the loss of something. Therefore, many firms are changing their partner compensation systems to reward partners for implementing the firm's strategic plan. Since most firms have unique strategic plans, they also have unique compensation systems. The keys to a successful partner compensation system are that the partners perceive the system as being relatively fair and trust those administering the system.

Changing attitudes requires education, time, thinking and planning. There are five things you can do in the next 90 days that will have a major impact on the firm culture and long-term profitability.

1. Develop a strategic plan that is consistently communicated to employees and other stakeholders. Involve managers and future leaders.
2. Hold partners accountable in support of the strategic plan.
3. Evaluate, and if necessary, change the partner compensation plan.
4. Implement or enhance the support for a learning/training culture.
5. Evaluate your billing practices (rates, timing and value of services).

While these are not silver bullets, together they will have a positive impact on your firm and the future of its employees.

Part IV

PERFORMANCE³

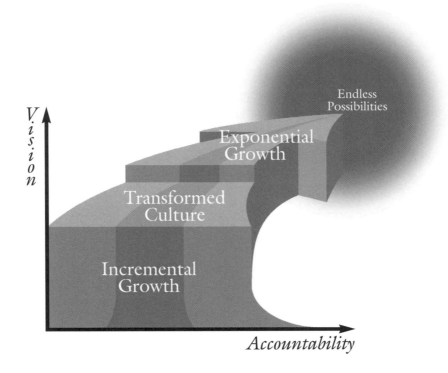

PLANNING × PEOPLE × PROCESS

Exponential Growth
Transformed Culture
Incremental Growth

Chapter 17

EXPONENTIAL RESULTS — 10 TIMES GROWTH

Incremental growth happens, even to poorly managed firms. *Exponential* growth, however, must be planned. It won't happen without great leadership, management and a shared vision.

It is alarming how many firms don't have a strategic plan. According to a recent survey, less than 1/3 of all firms reported have a strategic plan. Of those firms that do, less than half share the plan with employees. This is a startling statistic, and one that must be changed in order for firms to grow exponentially.

There are no "silver bullets," but simply spending time with your partners and managers can produce exponential results. In fact, growth in excess of 20% compounded annually is possible without acquisitions in some firms and markets if partners will simply pay attention to a few key indicators and examine their clients' dangers, opportunities and strengths. Those key indicators are:

- Revenue per full-time equivalent
- Per cent chargeable
- Technology investment as a % of net revenue
- Net income before owner's salaries
- Number and dollar amount of proposals in the pipeline

Like your golf handicap, the focus should be on improvement rather than peer statistics. Granted, it is interesting to know peer firm statistics, but the important statistics are your own. How can you improve and develop an exponential growth strategy if you don't know your own statistics? Sadly, many partners don't and may be managing using outdated measurements such as chargeable hours and utilization. It is easy to get caught in the trap of working *in the business* rather than *on the business*.

In order to achieve exponential growth, firms must implement effective leadership, management and a culture than supports growth. Leadership and management skills are different, but too often people assume they are comparable in the personal services industry. Great leaders are typically equipped to communicate a vision that others want to follow. Great managers, on the other hand, are charged with insuring that subordinates have the necessary resources and training in order to achieve the vision. From our experience, the majority of great managing partners or CEOs are leaders with a clear vision. Accordingly, the trend in today's personal service firm is to hire and develop managers who share the firm's vision.

The idea of management is often confused with managing client accounts versus managing people and other resources. While there are numerous leadership programs available, there are very few management programs that teach the following management skills:

- ❏ Team Building
- ❏ Accountability
- ❏ Delegation
- ❏ Pricing Services
- ❏ Attracting/Retaining People
- ❏ Risk Management
- ❏ Planning/Budgeting
- ❏ Client Filtering
- ❏ Time Management
- ❏ Web based tools
- ❏ Creative Problem Solving
- ❏ Improving Communications
- ❏ Project Management
- ❏ Performance Evaluation
- ❏ Process Improvement
- ❏ Training/Learning
- ❏ Meeting Management
- ❏ Five Star Client Service
- ❏ Process Improvement
- ❏ Mentoring versus Coaching
- ❏ Succession

In the past, successful partners and managers have acquired these skills from experience. But often they have not had the necessary training and experiences to *excel* as a great manager. Thus, they are limited in their capabilities to leverage and increase the return on their investments. While some may be satisfied with incremental growth, others are driven to achieve exponential growth. The PERFORMANCE³ Management Program offers training for managers in all areas of the firm (i.e. administration, tax department, audit department, technology and human resources).

What is a culture of growth and why is it important in order to achieve exponential growth? A culture is a system of shared beliefs. Common beliefs about goals, values and behaviors are required in order to achieve a firm's vision. Culture is strategic and directly affects everyone in your firm. Although it is often inherited, it can change if required to do so.

Firms can be successful with shared services, but it is impossible to move the firm from generation to generation without a shared vision. In today's growth environment, firms are learning that maintaining a culture through mergers and acquisitions is difficult. For these merged entities to achieve long-term success, they must have a shared vision and supportive culture. With that in place, firms position themselves to enter the third level of exponential growth and unlimited possibilities.

- Level 1 - firm improvement through better planning, people & processes
- Level 2 - improved culture with the one-firm approach
- Level 3 - exponential growth and unlimited possibilities

All of these stages require an investment in thinking and planning— something which most firms do not place enough emphasis. Without integrating personal with firm goals, it is impossible for firms to communicate significance and value to individual owners and employees. Without significance it is impossible to retain and attract the best and brightest talent.

You may be able to grow through mergers and acquisition, but is this a sustainable option? Do you acquire the best and brightest people? Not if you don't have a shared vision and a growth culture. Without a shared vision, firms will ultimately disintegrate at the top as partners compete among themselves for clients, resources and political power within the firm. It has happened in the past, is currently happening in some consolidations and, in my opinion, will happen in too many other firms if they don't take action to change their cultures sooner rather than later.

Yes, I said *change their cultures*. Every firm has a culture — whether it is good or bad. While every firm's culture is distinctive and in some ways unique, several characteristics differentiate firms that survive from one generation to the next (as opposed to those that are acquired or go out of business.)

Some of those cultural characteristics and beliefs are:

1. The firm is more important than any individual.
2. The owners have a shared vision.
3. Leadership is capable of building consensus.
4. The compensation system is tied to the firm's strategic plan. Honest and straight forward peer reviews at the owner level are conducted regularly.
5. The compensation system is viewed as fair and trusted by the owners.
6. Teams service clients and team members rotate to insure knowledge transfer and client satisfaction. The value to the client is the firm and not just the individual. (This requires a constant "ego check" by most partners.)
7. Long term objectives are important for the perpetuity of the firm.
8. Learning and training is a two-way street with support from firm leadership.
9. Core beliefs and values stay during major changes in strategy and organization.
10. Employees are just as important as clients. You can't attract and retain quality clients without quality employees and visa versa.

First generation firms struggle to build an enduring organization. Most do not survive the challenge. Why? Because building a firm that lasts generally requires an investment (sacrifice in profits) by the founders in addition to delegating client responsibilities and firm management. Being managed by another is not easy for many professionals and owners of professional service firms. However, doing so is liberating and allows the professionals to focus on their unique abilities.

Culture can be a key competitive advantage — or it can work against your firm. You must start from where you are today. The road ahead is up to you and your associates; however, there are some important first steps that will give any firm a quick start. The most important steps are:

1. Develop a shared vision strategic plan, soliciting input from owners, managers & staff.
2. Evaluate your system of governance and select the right leader(s) and manager(s). Support that leader with his or her management team. Some of your existing management team members may have to be replaced.
3. Make sure your compensation system rewards owners for focusing on the firm's strategic initiatives.
4. Utilize 90-Day Game Plans for everyone in the firm.
5. Hold everyone accountable, including the managing partner. (90-Day Accountability Reviews)
6. Foster a learning/training culture where people can grow throughout their career. Don't expect quality talent to do the same thing for an entire career. Lifetime learning and growth make for a rewarding career.

Managing a firm requires time, organization and the desire to insure that others succeed. It is not just about managing a book of business or client projects. It is about insuring personnel have the training and resources to succeed. Many partners provide lip service, but few walk the walk when it comes to managing people.

You should expect some conflict and challenges. If your firm doesn't have some tension, it may not have a noticeable pulse. That is the nature of a professional services firm. You can expect tension among:

- Partners, because they are competitive
- Generations, because they have different needs and desires
- Client teams, because they have different clients and team members
- Employees, because they have goals that sometimes compete with firm goals

Your firm's culture will determine how you handle these tensions. Too often partnerships ignore these tensions until the firm and individuals have been damaged. Culture is a stronger force than any partnership or shareholder agreement because it fosters an emotional commitment from owners and employees. It is also the second step to exponential growth and unlimited possibilities. Culture will bind your firm, its strategy and top performers together. Don't ignore this important competitive advantage; create it!

Creating the vision for exponential growth is important, and you can expect resistance from partners, managers and staff. Change is uncomfortable and it is easier for many to live with the now rather than risk for a bigger future. In order to create the culture and environment for exponential growth, you should ask the following types questions:

1. What should firm revenues be within three years? $_____
2. What should be the firm's revenue goal per FTE? $_____
3. How many owners will the firm have within three years? _____
4. What new markets do we want to enter?
5. Do any existing owners plan to leave or retire? _____
6. How many additional FTE's will be required? (Additional revenue divided by revenue per FTE) _____
7. To what new revenue opportunities should the firm allocate resources? _____
8. To what existing services areas should the firm reduce resources? _____

We have found the use of an audience response system provides honest and expedited results. Some people are hesitant to express their true feelings by a show of hands or by completing a paper survey. Questions designed using a Likert scale (1-10 disagree or agree) are generally effective in determining areas where more communication is needed in order to gain consensus and develop strategies to overcome obstacles.

The old saying that you can't get there from here is also often true when it comes to exponential growth. Firms should filter out both employees and clients who do not live up to the level of excellence demanded by the firm's core values and vision.

In summary, the following characteristics are required in order to achieve exponential growth:

1. A shared vision and strategic plan.
2. Great leadership and management.
3. A growth culture.
4. A training/learning culture
5. An employee and client filtering system.

The 80-20 rule applies. Eighty percent of firms are stuck in the incremental growth mode. Of the 20% that remain, 16% are transforming their cultures and 4% have reached the exponential growth and unlimited possibilities level.

At what level do you wish to play?

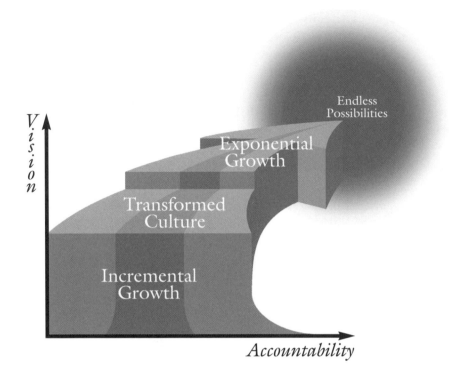

PLANNING × PEOPLE × PROCESS

Exponential Growth
Transformed Culture
Incremental Growth

Chapter 18

10 RULES OF
TECHNOLOGY MANAGEMENT

With the scarcity of qualified and experienced staff, the importance of technology continues to grow in today's accounting firm. Firms simply must do more with fewer people while raising production to offset increasing labor costs. In order to do so, they must either terminate less desirable clients or focus on improving their processes and technology. Perhaps your firm needs to do both? This requires a significant change in thinking, especially in those partners who have not been involved in firm management over the past few years and tend to only think about client service. Are they really providing good client service or simply maximizing cash flow as they burn themselves and staff members out trying to service clients that are marginally profitable? Review of current processes and the status of the firm's technology may hold the answer to these questions. The answers to these questions are not easy and sometimes are not the answers partners want to hear.

In an attempt to answer the questions and clarify what partners need to know about technology, I have put together ten rules of technology management. Partners do not need to know how to build the watch, but they do need to know how to tell time. Simply knowing these rules will not make a partner a technology guru, but it will enable them to participate in the development of a technology strategy for their firm as well as provide good advice to clients.

1. Technology is a strategic asset.
Many people, especially accountants, often try to manage technology as though it were overhead. This approach ensures frustration due to the fact expectations are always greater than the results based upon the resources committed. It makes more sense to manage technology strategically and allocate resources in accordance with priorities. Technology is an accelerator.

2. Professional technology skills are required.

Don't expect to get extraordinary results if you are not willing to invest in professionally trained personnel and/or outsource. Many firms make the mistake of thinking they need to hire someone who knows accounting to manage their technology. Often they get a marginal accountant who has marginal technology skills. Professional certifications and degrees in computer science are as important as a degree in accounting and passing the CPA exam. The breadth of technology has expanded until it is unrealistic to expect one person to have all of the technical skill sets as well as the ability to communicate with management and end users. Sourcing of these services has increased over the past two years.

3. Technology is dynamic and the investments will be on-going.

Technology is changing more rapidly than it did in the 90s. In order to keep up, firms must invest more in process improvement and training. Due to continued labor shortages and the advancement of technology, highly profitable firms will continue spending 6-7% of net revenues annually for technology and support, including labor. The definition of technology continues to expand in most firms and now includes phone systems, bandwidth, scanners and copiers. You may think this is too high. Do you know what % of net revenue your firm is currently spending on technology? What would the incremental cost be to do it right and eliminate the frustration or enable your people to increase revenue per full time equivalent? These are questions that can only be answered when a firm implements a consistent accounting system for technology and holds people accountable for training and adhering to firm policies and procedures.

4. Training is required for personnel of all levels.

Training is the quickest way to increase your return on investment in technology and people. It is also a key to both attraction and retention of quality people. According to the Gartner Group, you save five hours for every hour of technology training. In other words, 20 hours of training will provide 100 hours of increased capacity. Metrics of Boomer Technology Circle™ member firms show that revenue per full-time equivalent increases considerably in firms with excellent training programs. The attitude and confidence level of firm members increase accordingly.

5. A network of peer firms will assist the firm in managing their own technology.

You don't have to re-invent the wheel. Many firms tend to think their technology people should have all of the answers. What is happening is that firms are re-inventing the wheel. Firms should be sharing resources and developing improved technology management systems. Technology personnel are often hesitant to look to the outside for fear management will think they are inadequate. Developing a network of peers and utilizing that network is a professional strength and competitive advantage.

6. Firms need a management system for technology.

Technology is the number two expenditure in most firms following labor and fringe benefits. Many firms don't realize this because they utilize *peanut butter accounting...spread it thin and no one knows what you are spending.* It only makes sense to adopt sound management practices in order to ensure a return on the technology investment. There are several components to the management system we utilize and teach. It basically comes down to people, planning and processes with technology acting as the accelerator.

7. Someone from the owner group must be responsible for technology.

Technology leadership and vision are an integral part of today's firm management team. The requirements for a CIO or Technology Partner are similar to those of a Managing Partner. The skills include: leadership, finance, marketing, human resources, business savvy, project management and finally technical skills. Firms that have someone with these skills who is also an equity owner tend to be more successful than those who simply have an IT professional without all of these skills. Most partners don't know what they don't know when it comes to technology; and in many cases, IT professionals are not included in the development of the firm's strategic vision.

8. Operate from a written technology plan.

Follow the advice you give clients. Firms should operate from a technology plan that integrates with the firm's strategic plan. If you don't have these plans in place, invest the resources and get them in place. (Remember: planning, people and processes.) Without a plan it is easy for firm's to get caught in the trap of investing time and resources in trends such as the latest PDA/phone rather than substantive technology projects like integrated financial reporting and content management.

9. The Internet will play an increasing roll in your delivery system.

The recent disasters have made firms re-think their business continuation plans. Bandwidth continues to increase along with accessibility. Firms now are adopting internet based content management solutions as well as tax applications. Control of the application on firm servers is not as important as the security of the data and control over the processes. Your firm should have an Internet strategy including client portals. This strategy should include objectives, delivery strategy and a revenue model. Today, all of the major software vendors offer web-based or web-enabled solutions. It is all about improved client services, cost of ownership, increased productivity and improved management and security.

10. It's what you don't know that may cost you.

Innovation prompts change and the tendency is to resist change. I suggest you read *The World is Flat* by Thomas Friedman in order to promote global thinking and learn how technology is changing the world as well as our profession. You will also learn that the current skilled labor shortage in the United States is not the case globally. The Internet has leveled the playing field. Are you in a competitive position or is creative destruction biting at your heels?

Conclusion

Value is added when you provide leadership, relationship and creativity. Leadership provides direction, relationship provides confidence and creativity provides new capabilities. All of these components are necessary in managing technology and your firm.

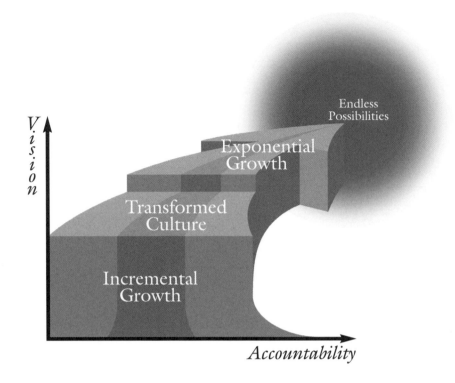

PLANNING × PEOPLE × PROCESS

Exponential Growth
Transformed Culture
Incremental Growth

Chapter 19

THE COMPENSATION CHALLENGE

Compensation of owners in a professional services firm has always been a contentious issue. Over the years several trends have developed based upon the size of the firm. A new trend, generally refered to as the Balanced Scorecard takes the best from previous systems and blends it with new developments in firm management. It is driven by the need to attain balance, accountability and promote teamwork.

It requires vision, strategy and time in order to properly implement. When most firm owners hear about the approach they become excited (positively and negatively) about its potential. *How is it going to affect my compensation* is the first and expected reaction. But few think about whether or not it's is going to be good for the firm. While this may be the normal state of affairs, it should not deter a firm from change. Change may be difficult, and it will likely take time along with plenty of communication to sell this important new vision. It is important to understand the evolution of compensation systems in order to move to the next level. Peer firm experiences can also be very valuable and save time.

Methods

First, let's quickly review the various compensation methods and comment about each. There are many variations, so don't be alarmed if your firm's system is a combination of two or more of these methods.

Equal	Easy and promotes mediocrity in larger firms
Formula Spreadsheet	The more complex the better in most firms
	Based upon the paper & pencil method, just automated.
Managing Partner Decision (MP)	CEO form of doing business
Compensation Committee	Works in large firms
Points/Units	Used in very large firms
Balanced Scorecard	New to the professional services firm

Motives

When speaking with partners from many firms, I discover many common motives. When I understand the thinking behind them I don't always agree with accompanying values and the results the systems produce. A good question to ask is, "Who is looking out for the firm?" Some of the terms I hear sound "bureaucratic" and subscribe to the "entitlement" philosophy. The following is a brief list of the most often stated motives:

- Fairness
- "Bottom line" driven
- Return on investment
- Objective versus subjective data (keep score with hard data)
- Leverage of resources
- Recognize seniority/experience
- One-firm concept
- Goal oriented
- Integration with the strategic plan
- *Results* based versus *effort* based

System – Usage – Tendencies

The following table shows where the various systems are typically used.

System	2-3 Partners	4-7 Partners	8-10 Partners	> 10 Partners
Equal	Common	Rare	Never	Never
Formula	Common	Very Common	Less Common	Seldom
Spreadsheet	Rare	Effective at upper end	Can Work	Too Difficult
MP Decision	Rare	Can Work Well	Becomes Difficult	More Difficult
Compensation Committee	No	No	Becomes Viable	Common
Points/Units	No	No	No	Still in Use
Balanced Scorecard	Will work in any size firm with proper leadership, governance and a strategic plan.			

Potential problems can easily be identified with each system, and firms tend to keep a system too long because of the fear of the unknown. Let's quickly look at these potential problems:

Equal

This system tends to work in newly created firms and those that have three or fewer partners. The system typically promotes mediocrity as the firm grows. Recall inequality comes from equal treatment of unequal people. This system can be extremely limiting to a firm's growth.

Formula

The biggest risk behind the formula system is that it often promotes the concept of sole proprietors sharing overhead rather than the one-firm concept. As such partners may hoard work and not leverage properly. This system also tends to overemphasize for technical skills and places little value on firm management, leadership, improved processes, vision and learning.

Spreadsheet

The spreadsheet system is quite similar to the formula system with the exception that it spreadsheet allows for more complexity. Accountants typically like complex formulas that are difficult for an outsider to understand. Perhaps this evolves from trying to get every owner's positive attributes included in the formula. Firms need a strategic plan or shared vision in order to make this or any of the systems work properly.

Managing Partner Decision

When firms possess a strong leader and visionary, the managing partner can successfully administer the owner compensation system. However, few firms are able to maintain this system. Typically the managing partner does not have a book of business or chargeable hours when this system is utilized.

The Compensation Committee

This is an attempt at balance and may come about when the managing partner does not want the sole responsibility for administrating the system. This system requires excellent communication and often is utilized due to the perception there isn't anything better. A compensation committee should be small, and the managing partner should be a permanent member of the committee. Other members should be elected. Not all owners should expect to participate on the committee.

Points/Units

This is the system most large firms use and is generally combined with the compensation committee. While the system may work, it has a tendency to overvalue technical skills and managed books of business. It can be the foundation for the Balanced Scorecard method, which we will discuss in more detail later.

One of the most disruptive results of all of these is the differences in compensation levels among owners with respect to the total amount of the compensation pool. Therefore, many firms have gone or are moving toward closed systems where partners do not know other partners' compensation. Typically owners can calculate approximate amounts in small firms with a limited number of owners.

The Balanced Scorecard

While it may be new to the accounting profession, it is not new elsewhere and has been employed in corporate American for over 10 years. The purposes of the Balance Scorecard are:

- Communicates strategy throughout the firm
- Informs owners/employees of how they fit
- Teaches owners/employees to focus on what is important
- Facilitates life balance
- Links firm and owners'/employees' success
- Provides feedback on a timely basis
- Rewards *results* rather than *effort*
- Provides opportunity for success at all levels within the firm

The Balanced Scorecard is typically arranged into four components: learning & growth, internal operations and processes, client development and satisfaction, and financial. The tendency of all companies (firms) who implement the Balanced Scorecard approach is to over emphasis financial measures. Accountants know how to measure financial results but have trouble with the other three components. Experts say financial results will come if proper focus is placed on employee learning and growth, improved processes and client development and satisfaction. Financial success is a result of other three.

By now you may have several questions. What is the Balanced Scorecard? Why are accounting firms interested? How do they use it? How do they implement it? We will attempt to answer your questions as we proceed.

The concept was developed at the Harvard Business School in the early 1990s by R.S. Kaplan and D.P. Norton. It is an organizational performance measurement system that has received widespread acceptance and is now being implemented by professional service firms. Some refer to it as a *pay for performance* system. The steps to the process are:

1. Clearly define business objectives and strategy.
2. Communicate measure, motivate and reward.

Obstacles are numerous and accountants are notorious for being able to identify the obstacles; but they don't often take the time to develop necessary strategies to overcome the barriers. Some of the more important obstacles are:

- Vision – inability to see and communicate what the future will look like.
- People – inability to attract and retain quality people.
- Management – inability to focus *on the business* rather than simply working *in the business.*
- Resources – with limited resources, firms must focus on a limited number of strategic objectives and initiates.   Often firms try to do too much and accomplish very little.

Vision

In most firms the employees fail to understand the business vision. It must be clearly and consistently communicated both internally and externally. Employees are the key asset in a knowledge based business. Communication and a proper understanding of the vision are critical to successful execution. Strategic goals must be translated into tasks, performance standards, and desired outcomes. Do not assume anything. It is much better for initiatives to be well-defined and consistently communicated.

People

In today's commoditized marketplace, it is becoming more difficult to retain and attract quality people. Compensation must be linked to performance and performance must be measured correctly. Employees tend to focus on what is measured, particularly if it is tied to compensation. The key measurement in the accounting industry is chargeable hours. Some will still argue this is a key indicator.

However, balance is necessary among financial, training/learning, process improvement and client satisfaction related initiatives. Compensation plans that reinforce the firm's strategic objectives are very important. The Balanced Scorecard should be cascaded down to the individual level. Reward employees for creating value. **Caution: start with the owner group before you apply the Balanced Scorecard to the staff. Wait at least one year before taking the system to the staff level. Solve problems at the owner level first.**

Management

Where is management focused? What is being measured? These are key questions in aligning management and the strategic plan. The management team needs to look beyond mere financial results. While these are important, so are investments in training/learning, processes, technology, and client satisfaction. With firms only averaging around 50% chargeable, there appears to be adequate time for other important initiatives. Management's responsibility is to balance conflicting priorities. Someone must provide the necessary leadership and discipline.

Resources

Resources must be budgeted and allocated in accordance with firm strategy. Without a strategic plan, firms often get caught in spreading too few resources across too many objectives and initiatives. Long-term goals must be balanced with short-term performance. Many firms get caught in the trap of maximizing current profits while avoiding necessary long-term investments in technology, re-engineered processes and training/learning.

Unfunded retirement benefits based upon owner salaries can be a detriment to making necessary investments. The firm should always come before any one partner's compensation or retirement plan. Be careful not to allow senior partners to over commit the firm to unfunded retirement benefits dependent upon future earnings. Everyone wants a great deal, but the firm must be able to excel and afford the benefits.

The Balanced Scorecard

A graphic of the Balanced Scorecard follows. Note that vision and strategy are at the core with the four primary perspectives linked.

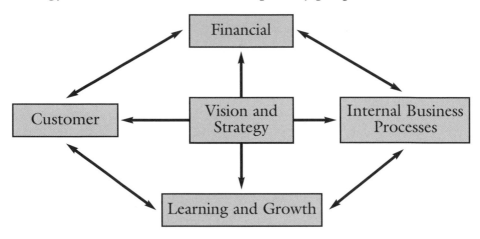

Each perspective can be valued differently depending upon the firm's valuation system. As a word of caution, make sure you give internal business processes, learning and growth, and customer satisfaction adequate value. In this example, we are assuming they are part of your firm's strategic plan. If not, then you will simply substitute your firm's strategic objectives.

Objectives and Measures

Establish *what* you are going to measure and then *how* you will measure. Most accounting firm's are comfortable measuring lagging indicators (or dealing with history). Leading indicators are just as important in managing a well run firm. Indicators such as client contacts, number of proposals outstanding and absenteeism are leading indicators. Cause and effect are most important when dealing with leading indicators. If...., then...., (else). Remember that goals are measurable while slogans are not.

What Next

If you think the Balance Scorecard approach has value for your firm, you should get additional training and do some research. Once this is complete, you will need to make the decision to take action and obtain buy-in from your partner group. This is never easy because partners tend to resist change. Their biggest question, even though they may not want to admit it, will be what effect it will have on their salaries. It will require a *trial run* to calculate what salaries would have been the past year if the system had been in place. Getting everyone striving for the same firm goals and completing their individual 90-day game plans will ensure success. Alignment and consensus are big factors in successfully implementing this approach. It is generally difficult for the managing partner (or any partner) to change a firm's compensation system. As such, it may require coaching from someone outside the firm. The saying that if you are part of a system, it is impossible to change the system holds true. It requires objectivity, education and confidence in order to ensure success.

Tips on Getting Started
1. Start with a strategic plan – without a plan you will have a weak foundation.
2. Don't start without total commitment from MP or CEO – leadership is a requirement.
3. Commitment is different than support – this is for all partners, not everyone but "me."
4. Use a facilitator/coach – it will reduce time and increase partner confidence.
5. Start with the partner group – do not include the staff the first year.
6. Use progress reports and 90-day game plans to reduce time – (simple tools that will reduce management time).
7. Schedule quarterly meetings in advance – meetings scheduled in advance have more importance.
8. Insure performance funds – financial rewards will change behaviors.
9. Focus on limited objectives – maximize your return by focusing resources on priorities.
10. Use graphics for positive visuals around the office – communicate consistently and often.

Sample Scorecards

The following scorecards are provided as examples of how firm objectives become owner and staff objectives. We recommend that you measure no more than five initiatives under each perspective. You will see in the example that we are only measuring three objectives. The objectives are weighed differently (importance) even though each perspective is assigned equal value. In this example, a maximum of 25 total points is assigned to each perspective. The score in each objective comes from quarterly evaluations. Firm success is tied to owner and staff success. The final score is reduced to a total value of 10 or less. This is only an example and your firm may chose not to weigh values. Most experts agree that each objective should not be equal in value; however, perspectives should be valued equally. The tendency of many owners will be to reduce values on everything but financial objectives. Each firm will have to determine its perspectives, objectives and values based upon its strategic plan. While this is only an example, you may find the objectives fit your firm with minor modification.

Conclusion

The Balanced Scorecard approach is new in the accounting industry. Few accounting firms have used it longer than two years. The system requires management's time and communication at all levels. If your current owner compensation system is not producing results that promote the one-firm concept, you should consider the Balanced Scorecard. It will hold owners accountable while spotlighting on priority objectives for the firm and individuals. It will also increase confidence as the firm grows and improves.

Sample Firm Scorecard

Sample Firm Balanced Scorecard

Perspective	Objectives	Weight	Points (Equal)	Score 1-10	Value
Financial	Increase revenue per FTE to $130k	10.00%	8.33	-	-
	Increase revenue by 15%	5.00%	8.33	-	-
	Increase NIBPS to 35%	10.00%	8.33	-	-
			25.00		-
Client Satisfaction	Complete satisfaction surveys on 33% of clients	10.00%	8.33	-	-
	Complete *New Opportunities Worksheet* on top 100 clients	10.00%	8.33	-	-
	Implement a client filtering systems	5.00%	8.33	-	-
			25.00		-
Internal Processes	Define unique processes in tax preparation	5.00%	8.33	-	-
	Implement a content management system	10.00%	8.33	-	-
	Outsource 300 tax returns	10.00%	8.33	-	-
			25.00		-
Learning & Training	Develop a learning curriculum for each employee	5.00%	8.33	-	-
	Hire a learning coordinator	10.00%	8.33	-	-
	Provide a training facility	10.00%	8.33	-	-
			25.00		-
	Firm Total	100.00%	100.00		-

Sample Partner Scorecard

Sample Partner Balanced Scorecard

Perspective	Objectives	Weight	Points (Equal)	Score 1-10	Value
Financial	Increase managed book to $1,000,000	10.00%	8.33	-	-
	Implement change orders in excess of $50,000	5.00%	8.33	-	-
	Manage head count to $130k per FTE	10.00%	8.33	-	-
			25.00		-
Client Satisfaction	Complete satisfaction surveys on 20 clients	10.00%	8.33	-	-
	Complete *New Opportunities Worksheet* on top 20 clients	10.00%	8.33	-	-
	Score all clients using the filtering system	5.00%	8.33	-	-
			25.00		-
Internal Processes	Serve on technology committee	5.00%	8.33	-	-
	Implement content management system	10.00%	8.33	-	-
	Identify & outsource 75 1040s	10.00%	8.33	-	-
			25.00		-
Learning & Training	Attend 40 hours of internal training	5.00%	8.33	-	-
	Complete securities licensing	10.00%	8.33	-	-
	Develop advanced Financial Reporting class with Learning Coordinator	10.00%	8.33	-	-
			25.00		-
	Partner Total	100.00%	100.00		-

Sample Staff Scorecard

Sample Staff Balanced Scorecard

Perspective	Objectives	Weight	Points (Equal)	Score 1-10	Value
Financial	Increase production to $175,000	10.00%	8.33	-	-
	Identify change orders in excess of $10,000	10.00%	8.33	-	-
	Acquire 5 new clients - $5,000 or greater	5.00%	8.33	-	-
			25.00		-
Client Satisfaction	Complete satisfaction surveys on 5 clients	10.00%	8.33	-	-
	Complete *New Opportunities Worksheet* on top 5 clients	10.00%	8.33	-	-
	Score all clients using the filtering system	5.00%	8.33	-	-
			25.00		-
Internal Processes	Serve on tax processing tax force	5.00%	8.33	-	-
	Convert files to electronic system	10.00%	8.33	-	-
	Identify 20 returns for outsourcing	10.00%	8.33	-	-
			25.00		-
Learning & Training	Attend 40 hours of internal training	5.00%	8.33	-	-
	Complete MOUS certification	10.00%	8.33	-	-
	Obtain CITP designation	10.00%	8.33	-	-
			25.00		-
	Staff Total	100.00%	100.00		-

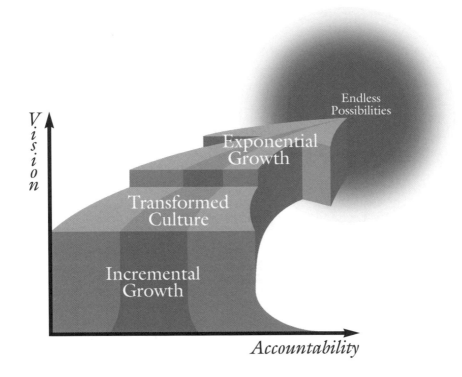

PLANNING × PEOPLE × PROCESS

Exponential Growth
Transformed Culture
Incremental Growth

Chapter 20

GRATITUDE AND CELEBRATION

Culture is a system of shared beliefs. Excellence can be a shared goal. These beliefs about goals, values and behaviors are required in order to achieve the firm's vision. Culture is strategic and directly affects everyone in your firm. It can be inherited, but it can change if required to do so. Firms can be successful with shared services. However, it is impossible to move the firm from generation to generation without a shared vision. In today's growth environment, firms are learning that maintaining a culture through mergers and acquisitions is not easy. For these merged entities to achieve long-term success, they must have a shared vision and supportive culture. With a shared vision and culture, firms position themselves to enter into the third stage of what we refer to as the PERFORMANCE³ Formula.

- Stage 1 - incremental improvement through better planning, people & processes
- Stage 2 - transformed culture with the one-firm approach
- Stage 3 - exponential growth and unlimited possibilities

These stages require an investment in thinking and planning, something most firms do too little of. Without integrating personal and firm goals, it is impossible for firms to communicate the significance of individual owners and employees. Without significance it is impossible to attract and retain the best and brightest.

You can grow through mergers and acquisition, but is it sustainable? Do you acquire the best and brightest people? Not if you don't have a shared vision and culture. Without a shared culture, firms will ultimately disintegrate at the top as partners compete among themselves for clients, resources and political power. It has happened in the past, is currently happening in some of the consolidations and in my opinion will happen in too many firms in the future if they don't do something to change their cultures sooner rather than later. Yes, I said change their cultures as every firm has a culture whether it is a good culture or a bad culture. While every firm's culture is distinctive and in some ways unique, there are common characteristics that differentiate the firms that survive from one generation to another from those that merge or go out of business.

Some of those cultural characteristics and beliefs are:

1. The firm is more important than any individual.
2. The owners have a shared vision.
3. Leadership is capable of building consensus.
4. The compensation system is tied to the firm's strategic plan. Honest and straight forward peer reviews at the owner level are conducted regularly.
5. The compensation system is viewed as fair and trusted by the owners.
6. Teams service clients and team members rotate to insure knowledge transfer and client satisfaction. The value to the client is the firm and not just the individual. This requires a constant "ego check" by most partners.
7. Long term objectives are important for the perpetuity of the firm.
8. Learning and training is a two-way street with support from firm leadership.
9. Core beliefs and values stay during major changes in strategy and organization.
10. Employees are just as important as clients. You can't attract and retain quality clients without quality employees and visa versa.

First generation firms struggle in building an enduring organization. Most do not succeed as it is challenging to say the least. It generally requires an investment (sacrifice in profits) by the founders and turning over client responsibilities and firm management to others. Allowing yourself to be managed is not easy for many professionals and owners of professional service firms. However, doing so is liberating and allows the professionals to focus on their unique abilities.

Culture can be a key competitive advantage or it can work against your firm. You must start from where you are today. The road ahead is up to you and your associates however, there are some important first steps that will give any firm a quick start. The most important steps are:

1. Develop a shared vision strategic plan, soliciting input from owners, managers & staff.
2. Evaluate your system of governance and select the right leader(s) and manager(s). Support that leader with his or her management team. Some of your existing management team members may have to be replaced.
3. Make sure your compensation system rewards owners for focusing on the firm's strategic initiatives.
4. Utilize 90-Day Game Plans for everyone in the firm.
5. Hold everyone accountable, including the managing partner. (90-Day Accountability Reviews)
6. Foster a learning/training culture where people can grow throughout their career.

Managing a firm requires time, organization and the desire to insure others succeed. It is not just about managing a book of business or client projects. It is about insuring personnel have the training and resources to succeed. Many partners provide lip service, but few walk the walk when it comes to managing people.

If your firm doesn't have some tension; it may not have a viable pulse. That is the nature of an accounting firm. You can expect tension among:

- Partners, as they are competitive
- Generations, they have different needs and desires
- Client teams, they have different clients and team members
- Employees, they have goals that sometimes compete with firm goals

Your firm's culture will determine how you handle these tensions. Too often partnerships ignore these tensions until the firm and the individuals have been damaged. Culture is a stronger force than any partnership or shareholder agreement. Culture creates an emotional commitment of the owners and employees. This is where the Gratitude shows – in the Pride of Ownership. It is also the second step to exponential growth and unlimited possibilities. Culture will bind your firm, its strategy and top performers together. This is worthy of genuine Celebration.

Don't ignore this important competitive advantage; create it!

L. GARY BOOMER

L. GARY BOOMER, CPA, CITP, CEO

Gary Boomer is the CEO of Boomer Consulting, Inc., an organization that provides strategic planning and consulting services to the leading firms in the accounting industry through The PERFORMANCE³ Process. Boomer strategies provide a transformation roadmap; team building and excellence while helping you make more money, attract quality people and grow your business.

Mr. Boomer is recognized in the accounting profession as the leading authority on technology and firm management. For the past ten years, he has been named by Accounting Today as one of the 100 most influential people in accounting. He consults and speaks internationally on management and technology related topics including strategic and technology planning, compensation and developing a training/learning culture. He acts as a planning facilitator, provides coaching and serves on many advisory boards.

He is the creator of and a facilitator for The Boomer Technology Circles™. Each circle is comprised of approximately 20 firms from unique geographic areas. The Circles meet three times per year and are connected through a private extranet. These circles help the best firms get better!

As an author, Gary has captured valuable knowledge in his book PERFORMANCE³. He is also the author of, Successful Technology Consulting… The Boomer Advantage and a contributor to The Boomer Advantage Guides Series. He also writes "Boomer's Blueprint", which is a regular column in Accounting Today and publishes the Boomer Bulletin™, a technology newsletter with international circulation.

Mr. Boomer received his BS and MS degrees in accounting from Kansas State University. He and his wife Mary have three children, Jeff, Jim and Katie.

BOOMER CONSULTING, INC.

BOOMER CONSULTING, INC.

Boomer Consulting Inc. provides strategic planning and consulting services to leading service organizations through the PERFORMANCE³ Process – People, Planning and Processes. Our strategies provide a roadmap for transformation, team building and excellence. Our unique processes include The Boomer Technology Circles, The Boomer Advantage Guides, and The Firm Summit, as well as technology and management related consulting services.

Most professional service companies focus on practice management techniques ranging form marketing to information technology. A revolutionary new way to differentiate business culture is the PERFORMANCE³ Process – simultaneously focusing on people, planning and processes. The unique focus on improvement, transformed culture and exponential growth, allows the company to continually make progress and move from one "level" to the next with unlimited future possibilities.

Focusing on any one best practice may result in incremental improvement. However, "Incremental" is just not enough in today's knowledge and wisdom based economy while "Exponential" growth is impossible without changes in mind-sets, strategies, skills, and tools.

Today we are watching as the world once again transforms to an age of wisdom. The decision your company must make; mediocrity or excellence? Will your company be satisfied with incremental growth or will they use the PERFORMANCE³ Process to experience true exponential growth?